HOW TO WRITE EAP MATERIALS

Julie Moore

TRAINING COURSE FOR ELT WRITERS

How To Write EAP Materials
By Julie Moore
This edition © 2020 ELT Teacher 2 Writer
www.eltteacher2writer.co.uk

Although every effort has been made to contact copyright holders before publication, this has not always been possible. If notified, ELT Teacher 2 Writer will endeavour to rectify any errors or omissions at the earliest opportunity.

Contents

ABOUT THE AUTHOR		5
1	INTRODUCTION	7
2	READING	19
3	WRITING	40
4	LANGUAGE WORK	60
5	LISTENING AND SPEAKING	86
6	WRITING BETTER EAP MATERIALS	108
COMMENTARIES ON TASKS		112
GLOSSARY		128

About The Author

After spending most of my twenties as an EFL teacher, first in Greece, then the Czech Republic, I realised that although I enjoyed trying to explain language, I wasn't really cut out for the teaching lifestyle. So I returned to the UK to do an MA at Birmingham University where I specialised in corpus linguistics and lexicography, and I found I loved playing around with words. That led onto a job as an ELT lexicographer at CUP working on learner's dictionaries and then a freelance career in ELT publishing.

I've continued to work on ELT dictionaries, but I also branched out, first into carrying out corpus research for other ELT authors and then into writing myself. I started off mostly writing supplementary materials, including workbook and other practice materials for series such as *New Inside Out* and *Global* (both for Macmillan), as well as two of the *Common Mistakes at ...* series (CUP) based on learner corpus research.

After a few years at my desk, I realised I was getting out of touch with the classroom, so I started teaching on summer, pre-sessional EAP courses at Bristol University, near where I live. A stint of a few weeks each year proved to be just the right amount of class time to reinvigorate my writing work and it also piqued my interest in the whole area of EAP and started to influence the direction of my writing.

My first experience of writing EAP materials was in-house at Bristol University, helping put together an in-sessional course using the university's VLE (virtual learning environment). Since then, I've gone on to write EAP grammar materials for *Macmillan English Campus,* I was senior editor on the *Collins COBUILD Key Words for IELTS* series and, combining two loves, I had a great time working on the *Oxford Learner's Dictionary of Academic English*. But I got my big break after sitting next to an editor from OUP at an EAP event, when I got involved in the *Oxford EAP* series of coursebooks, eventually co-authoring the Advanced/C1 level book with Edward de Chazal. Although I'd been involved in writing ELT materials for many years and I'd put together plenty of EAP materials for my own classes, writing classroom materials to be used by other EAP teachers turned out to be a surprisingly steep learning curve. The whole experience taught me a huge amount about both EAP and about writing EAP materials for others. Since then I've gone on to write two *Oxford Academic Vocabulary Practice* titles for OUP, as well as more IELTS materials.

1. Introduction

THE EAP CONTEXT

EAP[1] (English for Academic Purposes) can cover all manner of teaching contexts; from pre-university students to postgrads working towards a PhD, international students in English-speaking countries or those studying, wholly or partly, through the medium of English in other countries (sometimes known as EMI[2]). In this introductory section, we'll look briefly at some of the general issues you might need to consider before you even embark on writing anything.

Task 1

Before you start this chapter, here are a few questions to think about:

1. How many different EAP contexts – different types of students, types of courses, institutions, etc. – can you think of? Make a list.

2. In your own experience, to what extent do EAP materials you've used or come across cater for the needs of these different contexts (or not)?

---

[1] **EAP**
English for Academic Purposes: for students using English as a medium of study at university level

[2] **EMI**
English as a Medium of Instruction

7

3. In an ideal world, which factors do you think are most important to consider when writing EAP materials? List them in order of importance.

4. What potential restrictions do EAP writers face in catering for different EAP contexts?

You can read a commentary on this task on page 112.

Perhaps one of the most talked about differences in EAP teaching is between EGAP[3], English for General Academic Purposes, aimed at mixed groups of students from a variety of disciplines, and ESAP[4], English for Specific Academic Purposes, aimed at students studying in a single discipline, say medicine, law or engineering.

ESAP

If you're writing materials for an in-house[5] course aimed at students from the same discipline at a particular institution, you have the advantage of being able to co-ordinate, to a greater or lesser extent, with the target department. You may be able to gather course materials (such as set reading texts) as input, to find out about typical writing tasks, and maybe to sit in on lectures or seminars.

---

[3] **EGAP**
English for General Academic Purposes: aimed at students from any academic discipline

[4] **ESAP**
English for Specific Academic Purposes: aimed at students from a specific academic discipline, e.g. English for law students

[5] **in-house**
If you are writing materials for in-house use, they will be used within your own institution, not sold commercially. In terms of commercial publishing, in-house staff are those employed by the publisher, as compared with freelancers.

"Make sure your needs analysis is based on first-hand experience, not anecdotal evidence. For example, from time to time I teach dedicated in-sessional[6] courses at postgraduate level e.g. English for Economics, English for Food Science. This usually involves attending some modular lectures with the students, discussion with the relevant lecturers as well as colleagues who teach similar courses in other disciplines. This gives me first-hand (or nearly first-hand) experience of the demands on students studying on the related courses. This in turn helps to inform my materials writing for EAP."

John Slaght, University of Reading – co-author of *EAS: Extended Writing and Research Skills* and *EAS: Reading*

If you're writing ESAP materials for wider publication, you still maintain the advantage of being able to choose input on relevant topics and to focus on relevant output genres[7] (e.g. lab reports). However, you need to be aware of possible different approaches and specialisms within the field; the content of an engineering course at one institution may be very different from the syllabus and options offered at another. And are you going to focus broadly on engineering, more narrowly on electronic engineering, or

---

[6] **in-sessional**
In-sessional language courses take place during the academic year, usually at the same time as students' other studies. Compare with **pre-sessional** courses which take place before students undertake their main course of study, for example during the summer, to prepare them for their studies.

[7] **genre**
A genre is a particular form or style of written or spoken text with its own particular features; such as a student essay, an academic journal article, a textbook, a lab report, etc.

more narrowly still on microelectronics or signal processing?

EGAP

For all kinds of practical and administrative reasons, many EAP courses consist of students from a range of different disciplines.

EGAP materials need to draw on texts (reading or listening) from a range of subject areas that will engage this mixed target audience. Topics from broadly social science disciplines, such as business, sociology or international development, tend to be most widely accessible as they refer to issues which most people can relate to on a general level. It is possible though, with a little creativity and carefully chosen texts and tasks, to use materials drawn from apparently more specialist subjects such as law or the sciences.

EGAP materials tend to focus on generalisable features and functions that are relevant across disciplines rather than on topics. Students from any discipline will need to be able to summarise, to cite from sources and to ask critical questions. We'll see plenty more examples of key features and functions in EAP throughout the chapter.

Another important feature of good EGAP materials is the need to explicitly encourage students to relate what they are learning to their own discipline. This is the EAP version of 'personalisation' and is vital for developing learner autonomy[8].

---

[8] **learner autonomy**
Learner autonomy is the ability of learners to continue improving their own language skills independently, especially using skills and techniques learnt in class.

> "*Academic writing is enormously variable – across disciplines, across national academic cultures, and across institutions – and it's important to help students become aware of this variability. After presenting a 'model' of language use of any kind (e.g. the organisation of an essay introduction or referencing conventions), encourage students to reflect on or discover how things are done in their own subject area, how things are done in other academic cultures they may have experience of, and even (if appropriate) in their own academic department. Do these vary from the model? If so, how?*"
>
> Martin Hewings, University of Birmingham
> – author of *Cambridge Academic English B2* and *Advanced Grammar in Use*

EMI

Increasingly, universities around the world are choosing to teach wholly or partly though the medium of English. The motivations for this shift are various – sometimes it's to better equip domestic students for the more international nature of the jobs market, sometimes by offering courses taught in English institutions are able to attract a more international student body. As a materials writer, it's useful to be aware of the different role that English can play in an EMI context. Especially at institutions where students largely share the same L1, English may be used to varying degrees. Lectures and seminars may be in the L1, for example, but written work might be done in English, with reading texts drawn from a mix of L1 and English sources. This will obviously affect the mix of skills that these students need. Also in an EMI context, academic norms and conventions may be more influenced by the academic culture of the particular country or region rather than following the style and conventions expected in, say, a UK or US context.

Language level and **academic level**
As well as considering the general language level[9] of the students you're aiming at (Intermediate/B1, Upper Intermediate/B2, Advanced/C1+), you also need to take into account their academic level[10] (pre-university, undergraduate, postgraduate or maybe even postdoc or academic staff). How familiar are they already with their own subject area or with academic norms and conventions? Some students may have a jagged profile[11], for example a PhD student may be an expert in their subject area but have a relatively low level of English, while a new undergraduate may have a high level of general English but very little knowledge of what to expect in an academic context. EAP materials need to take these possibilities into account and avoid making assumptions about students' existing knowledge base.

---

[9] **language level**
A student's language level is their general level of language knowledge and ability, usually judged on a scale such as Intermediate, Upper Intermediate, Advanced, etc., or via a general language test (such as IELTS or TOEFL).

[10] **academic level**
A student's academic level is the stage they have reached in their academic studies, i.e. pre-university, undergraduate, or postgraduate.

[11] **jagged profile**
A student with a jagged profile has a high level of skill in some areas, but is much weaker in others, e.g. strong written English, but poor spoken skills, or good general English, but little academic experience.

Your Target Teaching Audience

As well as considering the general EAP context and the type of students your materials are aimed at, how you approach writing will very much depend on who you expect to teach the finished materials.

Many of us have written materials for our own classes, which we have used and adapted with varying degrees of success. However, just because something works well for you, doesn't necessarily mean it will transfer smoothly to a different teacher, with a different class, perhaps on a different course, or teaching at a different institution. When you create materials for your own classes, what you put on the page can be minimal; often just a source text plus a few prompts. You have in your head how you want to exploit the text, what you want to emphasise, what you might need to explain, how you want to organise activities, and you simply fill in any gaps as you go along. And of course, the materials are perfectly adapted to your teaching style, your students, and your teaching context.

Writing classroom materials to be used by other teachers, even for colleagues within your own institution, may require some of these gaps to be filled to make the material and its aims clear and coherent, while at the same time maintaining a degree of flexibility. It's important not to make assumptions about the knowledge, experience, style or approach of your target teaching audience. This will inevitably involve clear rubrics[12], consistent use of

---

[12] **rubric**
The rubric is the instruction that tells students what to do in a particular task or activity.

terminology[13], answer keys and teacher's notes. However, it's also important not to be too prescriptive. Skilled and experienced EAP teachers are very used to creating their own lessons and they won't want to be forced into an overly rigid, single route through a set of materials. Thus, there's a fine balance to be achieved between providing enough support for less experienced teachers, while at the same time creating materials that can be used flexibly by more experienced colleagues.

Task 2

Put yourself in the shoes of:

1. an experienced EFL teacher who is new to EAP

2. an experienced university subject lecturer who is new to ELT

3. yourself in your first EAP class

Consider what each teacher will need most from the materials they have to teach and what issues they might come up against.

You might consider terminology, language, classroom management, and content.

You can read a commentary on this task on page 113.

---

[13] **terminology**
In this context, terminology refers to the terms (words and phrases) that are specific to the teaching and learning of academic English. These could be linguistics terms (*noun phrase, clause, relative pronoun*, etc.) or academic terms (*thesis statement, stance, abstract,* etc.). See also **metalanguage**, which is the linguistic terminology used to describe and analyse language (*noun phrase, relative clause, adverbial*, etc.).

Issues, Arguments and Approaches in EAP

This chapter doesn't seek to address all the various issues, controversies and debates going on within the EAP community, nor does it set out to advocate any particular approach. It is, however, helpful to be aware of some of the topics which influence current thinking in the EAP world.

EGAP vs. ESAP

As our understanding of the nature of academic language has evolved, largely through corpus[14] research, some have argued that because the language, discourse[15] and genres typical of different disciplines vary so much, it makes no sense to teach general academic English. However, while there are strong arguments in support of teaching more focused ESAP courses that cater to the specific needs of students from particular disciplines, the reality for many EAP teachers is that they have to teach mixed groups out of practical necessity. This chapter will focus largely on writing materials for an EGAP context, but many of the principles are equally applicable to ESAP.

Authentic writing genres

Traditionally, essays have formed the backbone of EAP writing activities. However, research has shown that students are, in fact, required to write a range of different

---

[14] **corpus**
A corpus is an electronic database of language which is used to research usage. A corpus can represent the language as a whole or a specific area of language such as Academic English. Corpus research helps inform a lot of modern language teaching materials.

[15] **discourse**
Discourse is a general term to refer to all the features of language that are used to communicate in a particular written or spoken context. These can include vocabulary, structure, norms and conventions.

genres, such as reports, critiques[16], and proposals. So the argument goes that writing tasks in EAP should be more varied to reflect this. The distribution of genres that students might expect to encounter varies across disciplines, across levels of study and between institutions and even departments. Some university departments take a more innovative approach to coursework and assessment, including group tasks, reflective writing, portfolios and poster presentations, whereas others prefer a more traditional format. The essay, though, still remains the most common assessed writing genre overall.

It's perhaps also helpful to note that student writing genres are not the same as the texts written by professional academics (for textbooks or in journal articles). It's tempting to use reading texts as models for writing, but this isn't always helpful. The style of writing, the conventions and the range of vocabulary used by an experienced academic – not to mention all the work that happens during peer review and editing – are quite different from what is expected in an assignment from a student.

Low-level EAP

There's a general assumption that students come into EAP already having a basic grounding in general English. However, there is increasing demand, especially in some parts of the world, for students to enter EAP courses with very low levels of English. There's a trend towards introducing 'academic skills' into general English courses, or what is sometimes called 'soft EAP' or 'EAP lite'. Such courses introduce some of the principles of academic

---

[16] **critique**
A critique is a written or spoken evaluation of a text, a theory, method, case, etc. As a genre, critiques are a common form of student writing across disciplines, especially at higher levels. Also known as a *critical response* or *review*.

English (such as critical thinking[17] and basic academic vocabulary) and are aimed at pre-university students. However, it's questionable whether it's really possible to teach authentic EAP in a form that students will actually be able to use for university-level study at these low levels. This chapter focuses on materials aimed at students who already have at least a strong Intermediate (B1+, IELTS 5.5+, B2 First (FCE)) level of general English.

Language vs. study skills

Some argue that, especially on a short EAP course, it's more useful to equip students with the study skills[18] they will need to study in English rather than to try to work on their language (because little language progress can be made in such a short time). This has led to a largely skills-based syllabus that focuses on note-taking, reading techniques, etc., rather than traditional vocabulary and grammar. Others argue for a more balanced approach that includes work on both study skills and language. The challenge comes in integrating these elements effectively.

> *"Don't become obsessed with a particular approach even if it has proved successful in the past."*
>
> John Slaght, University of Reading – co-author of *EAS: Extended Writing and Research Skills* and *EAS: Reading*

---

[17] **critical thinking**
Critical thinking is the process of analysing, interpreting and evaluating information. It often involves asking critical questions about the accuracy, reliability or relevance of information in a written or spoken text, and making links between different sources.

[18] **study skills**
Study skills are the techniques and abilities that students need to develop for effective academic study. They might include, for example, the skills to read academic texts quickly and efficiently.

WHAT THIS BOOK DOES AND DOESN'T INCLUDE

This book doesn't set out to explain the specifics of how to write a reading activity or how to present and practise vocabulary, these skills are covered in other *ELT Teacher 2 Writer* titles (available from *eltteacher2writer.co.uk*). Neither does it go into detail explaining what academic English is, although it assumes some knowledge of concepts like *citation*, *thesis statements* and *noun phrases*.

It aims instead to highlight some of the issues that are specific to writing EAP materials, to suggest ideas and raise questions that you might not have considered. It draws on ideas from a wide range of published materials and tries not to advocate any particular style or approach, although I guess some bias is probably unavoidable. It also includes the thoughts and advice of several leading writers in the field of EAP very kindly contributed specifically for this chapter. Particular thanks to Fiona Aish, Olwyn Alexander, Sue Argent, Edward de Chazal, Martin Hewings, Sam McCarter, Louis Rogers, John Slaght, Jenifer Spencer and Jo Tomlinson.

2. Reading

Students in higher education need to read A LOT, so reading is unsurprisingly a key feature of any EAP course. Reading texts crop up in all kinds of EAP materials, not just to practise reading skills, but as input for writing and speaking activities, and also as a source of language-focused analysis and tasks, as we'll see in later chapters.

SELECTING READING TEXTS

The main sources for reading texts in EAP will be academic textbooks[19] and journal articles[20]. These can sometimes seem rather 'dry' or 'difficult' and it's tempting to choose more engaging, accessible texts on general academic topics from other sources, such as magazines like *National Geographic*, *New Scientist* or *The Economist*. These texts though are from a completely different genre, i.e. journalism, and their style and language exhibit wholly different, and indeed often opposite, features from academic writing. They use colourful language to bring their subject to life, they use informal, idiomatic language to draw their readers in and to make the content more familiar. They are also largely free from the restrictions of academic conventions around citing sources or carefully reporting evidence. For the learner coming from a general English background and trying to get to grips with the language, style and conventions of academic English, they

---

[19] **textbook**
A textbook is a book written specifically for students in a particular academic discipline to learn about their subject.

[20] **journal article**
An article published in an academic journal. These are often based on original research and are generally a more specialised, 'high-brow' genre than academic textbooks.

don't provide a helpful model. There's also the risk that students will pick up on marked language[21] and expressions from these texts which will stand out as inappropriate if used in their own writing.

> *"Teachers may be concerned that the content and vocabulary of [authentic] texts will present too many difficulties and should be left to a later stage, but the reality is that, for EAP students, there is no later stage. [...] Only if they are introduced to the forms and features of academic texts as early as possible can EAP students discover the difficulties they have to face and the strategies that might help overcome these."*
>
> Alexander, Argent and Spencer (2008)
> *EAP Essentials* p133

There are, however, a number of ways of using authentic academic texts that can make them more accessible to learners:

- texts written for lower academic levels will be simpler and more accessible, especially for learners with lower levels of English. You could, for example, use extracts from textbooks aimed at final-year high school students studying for A levels or for the International Baccalaureate (IB). Similarly, *Introduction to ...* textbooks for first-year undergraduates provide a useful source, also good for non-specialists in EGAP groups.

---

[21] **marked language**
Marked language is vocabulary that represents an unusual or stand-out choice by the writer or speaker. For example, a journalist might use a colourful idiom or a literary adjective to make an impact on their reader – the same vocabulary used in a student essay would stand out to a native-speaker reader as odd or out of place.

- introductions (to articles, chapters or sections) generally make good extracts because they give more background context than mid-sections. Similarly, abstracts[22] and other summaries work well as standalone texts. Discussion and conclusion sections of texts can work too, as they often recap the topic, but they may need a short intro to 'set the scene' in the rubric.

- adapting a text to make it simpler runs the risk of distorting the very features of academic English that we're trying to teach. Also, if students are to get to grips with the ideas and arguments in a particular text, too much adaptation risks misrepresenting the original author's points. It is possible though to choose a short section of a longer text or to abridge a text, leaving out details or sections that are not necessary for the task.

- glossaries can help students with tricky specialist vocabulary, concepts or cultural references.

- careful layout, bolding and highlighting can draw attention to target features, key words or main points.

- artwork, in the form of pictures, graphs or even infographics can be used to illustrate concepts within the text and help students get to grips with the content.

---

[22] **abstract**
An abstract is a short summary of the contents of a text. Abstracts appear at the start of academic journal articles and some longer pieces of student writing to give the reader a quick overview and to help them decide whether to read the full text.

COPYRIGHT AND CONVENTIONS

If you're using authentic texts in any materials, you need to be aware of restrictions around copyright[23] and getting permission[24] from copyright holders. All written materials, whether published in a conventional way, in books or journals, or online, are covered by copyright.

If you are producing materials for use in your own classes or for use within your own institution, you may be covered by a licence held by your institution (in the UK this will be from the Copyright Licensing Agency, *cla.co.uk*). You should check what licences your institution holds and any restrictions they include. Different legislation will apply in different countries. There will usually be restrictions on how much of a particular work you are able to copy and how widely it can be distributed. You may also need to complete some paperwork. Your university library will usually be a good starting point for information on copyright.

If you're producing material for a commercial publisher, it will usually be their responsibility to seek copyright permissions. As the author, you need to be aware of any restrictions they might have on the amount of copyright material you use – obtaining permissions can be time-consuming and expensive. You should also keep an accurate record of any sources you use with the full

---

[23] **copyright**
The person or organisation that owns the copyright of a text (or other published material) is the only person who has the legal right to publish it. If you want to reuse a published text, you must ask the copyright holder's permission.

[24] **permission**
If you want to reuse a published text (or other material) you must get permission from the copyright holder.

publication details. Check with your editor at the start of a project – it can be difficult to go back and track things down again once you've got started.

With more material, including academic texts, now available online, the use of creative commons[25] licences is growing. If material has a creative commons notice – indicated by the cc symbol – this means that the creators have specified particular rights of use, often making it freely available to be copied or adapted without the need to apply for permission. You can find out more about creative commons at *creativecommons.org*.

Regardless of your context and the situation re. copyright, you should always properly acknowledge the source of any text. Not least because if you're teaching students about the perils of plagiarism[26], you should be setting a good example yourself! For EAP materials, it makes sense to show source information at the bottom of a text using standard academic referencing conventions. This will also help your students get used to identifying and evaluating source information, such as how old a text is, whether it's from a reliable

---

[25] **creative commons**
If a text (or other published material) has a creative commons notice (indicated by the cc symbol), this means that the creators have specified particular rights of use, often making it freely available to be copied or adapted without the need to apply for permission. You should note however, that there may be certain requirements for attribution.

[26] **plagiarism**
Plagiarism is the use of someone else's work in your own writing without acknowledgement. It can involve using the exact words or ideas from another writer without a correct reference. Plagiarism is frowned on in academic contexts and may attract serious penalties (such as failing an assignment). See also **patch-writing**, which is where a student writer puts together sections of a text based on ideas from different sources but without linking them together in a coherent way.

academic source, etc. There are various different sets of conventions for citing and referencing (APA, MLA, etc.). Information about most of these can be found online or via your university library. The important thing is to decide which style you are going to use and stick to it.

READING ACTIVITIES

> *"Work out your learning objectives. Then research texts that you can use to achieve these, rather than finding a nice text and deciding what you can do with it. Construct a sequence of tasks that leads towards each learning objective. Each task should be necessary to reach the learning objective, but not sufficient in itself, so that it builds on previous tasks and leads into later ones."*
>
> Edward De Chazal
> – author of *Oxford EAP* and *English for Academic Purposes*

Reading activities in EAP can be broken down into four main types. A single text though may be used for activities in more than one of these categories and they will often overlap.

1. **Reading skills** – strategies to help students cope with the volume of reading they'll encounter in their studies.

2. **Text analysis** – understanding how an academic text is constructed and identifying typical features of academic writing.

3. **Language work** – using a text to provide examples of vocabulary or language forms typical of academic English.

4. **Content input** – a reading text can also provide input for other tasks.

Reading activities are typically presented in four stages: lead-ins, quick reading tasks, close reading and follow-up tasks.

Lead-ins

In the real world, we don't often come to a text cold. A student will read to find out more about a topic they're already studying, often as a follow-up to a lecture on the topic, so they'll start off with some background knowledge and expectations about the text. Lead-in tasks are a way of approximating this situation in the classroom, especially where the text is on an unfamiliar topic. They can function to:

- introduce the topic and give students the opportunity to establish and share their existing knowledge, especially in mixed-discipline groups.
- establish the meaning of key terms and vocabulary that will appear in the text.
- establish a purpose for reading the text.
- encourage critical thinking by getting students to raise critical questions around the topic before they start reading.

For example, a lead-in to a text about maps and mapmaking in *Cambridge Academic English Upper Intermediate* starts off by simply introducing the topic and relating it to students' own experiences. It uses pictures of different types of maps to bring the topic to life and to give students a concrete starting point for their discussion, asking about how they use different kinds of maps in their daily lives and how maps affect your view of the world. It then goes on to establish a purpose for reading – preparation for a tutorial – and also feeds in some key vocabulary that will appear in the text for students to check.

It's worth bearing in mind that in everyday life we tend to talk about real or concrete things (people, objects, places, events), while academic writing is often about more abstract concepts (theories, trends, arguments). So one way of making academic texts more accessible is to link those abstract concepts to concrete, real-world things and examples that student readers can relate to, such as the maps in the above example.

Another lead-in that I wrote for *Oxford EAP Advanced* introduces a text about how we define the concept of poverty. It uses a definition of poverty taken from the reading text to introduce the topic and check some key vocabulary. The definition is intentionally taken out of context in order to provoke critical thinking and discussion, asking students to consider how we define poverty in different contexts (i.e. in poorer or more affluent countries or areas). This is intended to encourage students to approach reading the text with critical questions already in mind.

The discussion questions in the above activity ask students to 'give reasons'. It's important for students in an academic context to explain and justify their ideas, so this is good practice. Look back at Task 1 – which similar devices did I use to make the reflective tasks here more active? Other useful rubrics for making discussion-type questions more structured and getting students to expand on or explain their answers include:

Give reasons / examples.
List / Note down x [reasons / advantages / factors].

Agree on the [three most significant factors].
Rank the [factors / criteria] in order of importance.

Quick reading tasks

Academic readers will often have to plough through large amounts of reading material, deciding what is most relevant or useful for them at that time and so what to focus on. Proficient academic readers don't typically read a whole article from start to finish, but jump around picking out the 'juicy' bits, often going from the introduction straight to the discussion and conclusion. Thus, developing strategies to navigate[27] texts and improve reading efficiency is vital. Activities that encourage skimming[28], scanning[29] or quick reading are often closely linked to the reason for reading the text.

Giving students a final task focus up front can be helpful in directing their purpose for reading. Typical tasks might include reading a text:

- as part of research for an essay / presentation on a given topic.

- to write a summary (of the text, of a process described in the text, or for a literature review).

---

[27] **navigate**
When you navigate a text, you find your way around it efficiently to find the information you need, for example making use of abstracts, content pages, headings, etc.

[28] **skimming**
Skimming is a reading technique in which you read a text quickly to pick out the main points, ignoring details.

[29] **scanning**
Scanning is a reading technique in which you scan a text for specific information, for example searching for a particular key word or phrase.

- to prepare for a discussion on a given topic.
- to write a review / critique.

Note that the task can be one that students will actually complete (see *Follow-up tasks* below) or it could be a hypothetical task just to give a focus to the reading process.

Questions that might be raised at this stage include:

1. Is this a reliable source?

- tasks that involve identifying the source of the text; the genre, audience, purpose, date, etc.
- tasks to develop information literacy[30], such as evaluating the reliability of online sources

2. Is this text relevant to my topic/assignment?

- tasks that involve identifying topic and key themes
- making use of titles, abstracts, contents pages, key words and headings

Remember that all the 'noise' that surrounds academic reading can be confusing for many students who are used to reading in an EFL class, working on simple texts word-by-word and checking unknown vocabulary. Exposure to lists of contents, abstracts, headings, references, footnotes, etc. is also important to help students navigate academic texts to find the information that is relevant to their purpose.

---

[30] **information literacy**
Information literacy is the ability to find, evaluate and effectively use information relevant to a task. It is particularly relevant to EAP students searching for information either online or in a university library.

3. How does this text fit in with my other knowledge?

- tasks that focus on identifying key arguments, the perspective of the text, the author's thesis and/or stance[31]
- techniques that involve identifying and using topic sentences, identifying key recurring terms and phrases, and ignoring details, such as references, data, etc.

"Balancing the challenge of the task type and text is important. Arguably, if you have an easier text you can push the students with more challenging tasks."

Louis Rogers, University of Reading – co-author of *Oxford EAP B1+* and *Delta Academic Objectives*

Students new to EAP will need support to pick out this key information. Giving multiple-choice options to choose from initially will give them a starting point. This support can gradually be reduced as students become more familiar with academic texts and principles. Thus each of the tasks below might be appropriate at different stages of a course, with different types of students or different types of text:

A Choose the statement which best expresses the author's stance.
a. The author believes that this approach can be effective and economically viable.
b. The author questions whether this approach is cost-effective.
c. The author criticises this approach as inappropriate and ineffective.

---

[31] **stance**
A writer's stance is the position they take on the topic they're writing about; an academic point of view.

> **B** Which phrase best describes the author's stance? Give reasons for your choice.
> a. *broadly supportive of the approach*
> b. *sceptical about some aspects of the approach*
> c. *highly critical of the approach*
>
> **C** Briefly summarise the author's stance.

The way you present a text on the page, using highlighting, bolding, labelling key features, etc. can also help students get to grips with it. In a reading text I used in an early unit of *Oxford EAP Advanced*, I presented a text with the topic sentences[32] in bold, the sentences which explained and expanded on the key ideas (supporting sentences) in plain text and then the detailed evidence, references, etc. in grey text. This serves to break down a long and rather daunting text into more manageable chunks very visually. In the first activity, students are asked to read only the bolded topic sentences in order to establish the key arguments. This shows them that they can understand the basic ideas in the text without having to plough through all the details (and mimics the way that many academic readers skim through texts). It also serves to demonstrate how a typical academic text is constructed, with each paragraph moving from general to specific.

Quick reading tasks might also encourage students to explicitly work on reading speed, by timing how long it takes them to read a text and calculating their words-per-minute (see, for example, Slaght, 2012, p31).

---

[32] **topic sentence**
A topic sentence usually appears towards the start of a paragraph and expresses the main topic of the paragraph. Other sentences in the paragraph further explain or support this main idea. Note: while the idea of the topic sentence can be a convenient teaching tool, not all linguists agree about the concept.

Close reading tasks

Close reading tasks, in which students focus on specific features of the text, usually make up the main part of a reading lesson and they should be closely linked to the syllabus aims. The list below is far from exhaustive, but suggests some of the areas that reading tasks might focus on:

Rhetorical functions – *what* the writer is trying to achieve in a text

- setting out a purpose / thesis / research question
- describing / reporting on a process, case study, research, etc.
- presenting an argument + explanation / supporting points + evidence
- incorporating evidence (especially data, graphs, etc.)
- setting out alternative arguments / perspectives
- describing cause and effect relationships
- setting out problem + solution + evaluation
- expressing stance and perspective
- expressing evaluation / critiquing
- summarising

Features of academic style – *how* the writer achieves their aim

- structure – of whole texts and individual paragraphs (general to specific patterns)

- hedging[33] – through confident and tentative language choices
- impersonal language – use of non-human subjects and passives
- coherence and cohesion – linking ideas together logically, avoiding repetition
- citing and referencing conventions
- register[34] and academic vocabulary
- using language concisely, e.g. through long noun phrases

Critical thinking – how the reader *reacts* to the text

- asking critical questions
- identifying assumptions
- evaluating evidence and arguments
- linking a text to existing knowledge and a wider context
- comparing ideas across texts
- synthesizing information

---

[33] **hedging language**
Hedging or hedging language is used to soften the impact of a statement or claim, making is more cautious or measured. Modal verbs (*could, may, can*) and adverbs (*approximately, typically, sometimes*) are typical examples of hedging language.

[34] **register**
The context in which language (esp. vocabulary) is most typically used can be described as its register; the tone or style of the language, e.g. formal, informal, technical, literary, etc.

Task 3

Match the text types / sections below to the features of academic writing they might best be used to illustrate.

For example, you might choose a *description of a process* to look at *impersonal language*.

Text type
abstract
article / chapter introduction
literature review
description of a process
results section
discussion section
article / chapter conclusion

Feature to illustrate
referencing conventions
hedging language
expressing evaluation
expressing stance and perspective
purpose and thesis statements
impersonal language
expressing sequence / chronology
rephrasing and summarising
data commentary

You can read a commentary on this task on page 114.

Students new to EAP will need a lot of guidance and examples when they start to analyse texts. So, you might use colour-coding or labelling to highlight the main argument, supporting arguments and evidence in one paragraph, then ask students to break down the following paragraphs in the same way. Critical thinking may be unfamiliar to some students, especially those from cultures where questioning received ideas is not encouraged. So again, students will need clear guidance and scaffolding[35] in initial critical thinking tasks. In *Cambridge Academic English Upper Intermediate*, for example, six claims are underlined and labelled within a short text and students are given critical questions to ask about each claim. They have to consider whether each claim is fact or opinion and whether it is supported by convincing evidence. They are also asked whether they agree with the opinions expressed, an important first step towards developing their own stance.

As a course progresses and students become more familiar with analysing texts in this way, questions can become more open and less supported. Towards the end of a course, focus should shift more towards the purpose for reading and the end task, leaving students to figure out for themselves which reading and analysis techniques will be most useful in order to achieve their aim.

> *"Ideally make tasks student-centred, so they have some responsibility to actually do something with the material. Build in some unkeyability (i.e. tasks that don't have a simple answer in the key), open-endedness or personalisation."*
>
> Edward De Chazal
> – author of *Oxford EAP* and *English for Academic Purposes*

---

[35] **scaffolding**
The support that you provide for students in completing a task, for example, several stages or activities which lead towards a final aim, is known as scaffolding. More difficult tasks, or tasks early in a course might need more scaffolding to guide students step by step.

Follow-up tasks

After close analysis of a text it's often useful to widen out the focus again to a more global task. It's easy for students to become bogged down in the details and to lose sight of the overall message of a text. They sometimes need to step back to see how the writer's ideas are connected and how these connect to other ideas outside of the text.

> *"Nested layers of themes in sentences, hyper-themes in paragraphs and macro-themes in whole texts work together to manage the development of ideas through a text."*
>
> Olwyn Alexander, Heriot-Watt University
> – co-author of *EAP Essentials* and *Access EAP*

A follow-up task might refer back to a purpose set out at the start. It may be a relatively short activity to round off the lesson, such as a set of general discussion questions, or a written or oral summary.

In a mixed-discipline group, follow-up tasks can also be used to help students relate what they've explored in class to their own discipline. For example, if you've been analysing the use of references and referencing conventions in a text, a follow-up task might involve getting students to investigate which referencing conventions are most commonly used in their own discipline. To avoid these tasks becoming throwaway homework activities, it's helpful to include concrete follow-up activities, where they report back to the class on what they find, a valid academic skill in its own right.

Alternatively, the text (or texts) might be used as input for another lesson. As we will see in later sections, it's important to use real academic content to feed into writing and speaking activities in order to give students something solid to write or speak about.

Task 4

Look through any EAP materials you have to hand:

1. How many different tasks or activities are directly linked to one reading text?

2. How do they fit into the four stages above?

3. Are the reading texts used as input for other skills?

What advantages and disadvantages might there be in reusing a reading text as input for an extended writing or speaking activity, for example in the next lesson?

You can read a commentary on this task on page 115.

Reading Materials Checklist

Aims

- Does your reading activity have a clear aim; what will students take away from the activity (e.g. a better understanding of how writers use evidence to support their arguments)?
- Is your aim explicitly stated (to students and teacher), for example, in a rationale[36]?

Text

- Is the reading text authentic; is it of a style and genre that students might encounter in their academic studies?
- Have you checked the copyright situation re. any texts you use?
- Is the length and complexity of the text appropriate for the target students?
- Is there enough background information so that the extract makes sense in isolation and to a non-expert reader?
- Would a glossary[37] or some artwork help students deal with the text?

---

[36] **rationale**
A rationale is a written statement of the reasons for doing a particular activity and the outcomes it hopes to achieve.

[37] **glossary**
A list of terms and definitions. Glossaries can be used with reading texts to help students with difficult terms, vocabulary or cultural references.

Activities

- Does the lead-in help students relate abstract ideas in the text to concrete, real-world ideas or experiences, to get a handle on the topic?

- Do students have a clear purpose for reading?

- Is the overall task appropriately scaffolded, so that there are enough manageable steps to guide students through each stage of understanding and analysing the text? Remember teachers with a stronger group can always skip over some steps, but weaker students will be discouraged if each step is too challenging.

- Is there a balance of activities that look at the text globally (main points, perspective, author's stance, etc.) and in detail?

- Can you integrate some language work into analysis of the text?

- Have you pushed students to explain or support their answers?

- Do the activities involve an element of critical thinking at each stage so that students really engage with the text and don't just look at the surface meaning?

- How can you round off the activity, e.g. a summary of the text, a discussion question, a reflection on the reading skills or text features, a link to other disciplines?

CHAPTER REFERENCES

Alexander, Argent and Spencer (2008) *EAP Essentials* Garnet Publishing: Reading de Chazal and Moore (2013) *Oxford EAP Advanced/C1* OUP: Oxford

Hewings and McCarthy (2012) *Cambridge Academic English Upper Intermediate* CUP: Cambridge

Slaght (2012) *English for Academic Study: Reading* Garnet Publishing: Reading

3. Writing

The leap from writing in a general ELT class to academic writing is perhaps one of the biggest that students new to EAP have to make. Students' previous experience of writing in English is likely to have been fairly short tasks aimed primarily at practising or demonstrating their language skills. Provided they displayed a good range of vocabulary for their level, reasonably accurate grammar and threw in a few nice discourse markers, a fairly vague essay which said nothing very much of substance could probably have gained them a good grade. Writing in an academic context is far more rigorous, demanding both accurate and appropriate language, as well as meaningful and well-structured content. As one commentator remarks: 'After all, we teach college students to write not because we expect them to become writers, but because writing is the evidence that they are mastering intellectual concepts.' (McBride, 2012). Thus, EAP writing tasks should be aimed at helping students develop the skills they need to express intellectual concepts in a way that will do justice to their knowledge of their discipline and not sound like simplistic high-school essays.

GENRES AND STUDENT WRITING

The essay
Work on academic writing skills has traditionally focused around essay writing. This is partly because it's a genre that can encompass a range of writing skills in a single task (organisation, argument, evidence, synthesis of sources, discussion, evaluation, etc.), but also because it's a genre familiar to many EAP teachers, who tend to come from an Arts and Humanities, or Social Science background themselves, where they probably wrote plenty of essays in

their own university days. It's often argued by those in the ESAP camp, and by EAP students themselves studying in the sciences, that 'scientists don't write essays' and what they need is practice with lab reports or other technical documents. This is true to an extent, but research into the written genres produced by students across disciplines at four UK universities, using the British Academic Written English corpus (BAWE; *www.coventry.ac.uk/research/research-directories/current-projects/2015/british-academic-written-english-corpus-bawe/*) has shown that essays are, in fact, used across all disciplines, albeit to a lesser extent in the Life Sciences and Physical Sciences (Nesi and Gardner, 2012, p50–51). That's not to say that they should be the only genre practised in EAP materials, but there is still a good case for their inclusion, and they can provide a good basis for teaching key principles that can be applied to other genres.

Other writing genres
Interestingly, Nesi and Gardner (2012) found that the only other genre that occurred across all disciplines was the critique; which could take the form of an evaluation of anything from a book or a film, to a piece of legislation, a financial report, a product or a website. They found that, perhaps unsurprisingly, critiques became increasingly common at higher levels of study as students progressed from simply describing basic ideas and were expected to employ higher-order thinking skills to interpret, analyse and then evaluate. The language of evaluation can be particularly tricky for EAP students, grasping the difference between personal opinion and informed comment, and getting the tone right in terms of being appropriately confident or tentative (via hedging language and vocabulary choice). So this is a really useful area to focus on, especially with students at or heading towards postgraduate level.

Other genres that are more restricted to particular fields (case studies, design specifications, methodology recounts, etc.) may be more tricky to tackle in materials aimed at mixed groups, although aspects of other genres can be practised in shorter writing activities as we'll see below.

Task 5

1. Make a list of the academic student writing genres you're familiar with, either from your own experience as a student or as an EAP teacher.

2. List genres you think might be specifically relevant to student writers in: biology, engineering, medicine, law

3. What possible challenges might you come up against in devising materials to teach more specialist academic writing genres?

You can read a commentary on this task on page 116.

To learn more about student writing genres there's a great section on the British Council website based on BAWE research called Writing for a Purpose (*learnenglish.britishcouncil.org/en/writing-purpose/writing-purpose*) – useful for students, teachers and materials writers.

The BAWE corpus itself is also available to search for free via Sketch Engine (*sketchengine.co.uk/bawe*). Searching for examples of student writing by genre and discipline can help you get a feel for the types of tasks and language that might be relevant to practise. Bear in mind though that the corpus is for research purposes only and specific examples should not be reproduced in teaching materials – see the University of Coventry website for more information about usage. A similar resource based on student writing at US universities is MICUSP (the Michigan Corpus of Upper-Level Student Papers) which also allows you to search for examples of student writing labelled by discipline and by paper type – available at *micusp.elicorpora.info*.

Short writing tasks

As well as activities that involve writing a complete essay, critique or report, short writing tasks can be particularly helpful in focusing on subskills which are relevant in a range of contexts. Short writing tasks might involve writing a single paragraph, either envisaged as part of a larger text (e.g. students write an essay plan + a single body paragraph) or as a standalone text (e.g. a summary). Some of the benefits of short writing tasks include:

- By focusing on a specific subskill (e.g. summarising, reporting from sources, commenting on data) students feel less overwhelmed by the task at hand.

- Short writing tasks can be done collaboratively in class, allowing for communication both between students and between teacher and students.

- Short tasks allow more flexibility for the teacher in terms of lesson planning and classroom management – a long build-up to a big task may be less easy to fit into a particular class length or timetable.

- Short tasks can allow for quick feedback and rewriting to improve successive drafts in a relatively short time.

- Shorter writing tasks can tackle some of the specific skills involved in the more difficult-to-practise genres (as mentioned above), such as data commentary, a description of a process etc., catering for less essay-focused disciplines, like the sciences.

- In mixed groups, it may be more practical to ask students to research a topic from their own discipline for a short task, e.g. to research a single graph to use as the basis for a data commentary or to choose a key term to define, allowing for an element of discipline personalisation.

Writing for assessment
Inevitably, a large amount of the writing that students will do through their studies will be assessed in some form, so EAP materials need to acknowledge this aspect of academic writing. This may involve work around:

- understanding the question, e.g. work on key verbs in essay questions; *discuss, compare, evaluate*, etc.

"It's worth spending quite a lot of time on simply analysing tasks. Students can often fall down not due to a lack of knowledge, but through their inability to understand exactly what they need to do."

Louis Rogers, University of Reading – co-author of *Oxford EAP B1+* and *Delta Academic Objectives*

- understanding and using assessment criteria
- raising awareness around norms and conventions, e.g. using university or department websites to check which referencing conventions to use
- raising awareness around issues such as plagiarism, patch-writing[38] and research ethics

---

[38] **patch-writing**
Patch-writing is where a student writer puts together sections of a text based on ideas from different sources but without linking them together in a coherent way. It may not constitute **plagiarism** (if everything is correctly acknowledged), but often suggests the student has not really

Non-academic writing
Some EAP materials also include work on the writing that students will do at university that is not directly academic, such as email communications with their department, tutor, etc. *Access EAP Foundations* (Argent and Alexander, 2010) is an example of a coursebook with a strong emphasis on student life and adapting to study at an English-speaking university. Because the norms and conventions of such communication vary greatly between different cultures, even between English-speaking countries like the UK and the US, such materials are much easier to write if you have a specific market / audience in mind.

APPROACHES TO TEACHING WRITING SKILLS

It's possible to approach the teaching of writing skills from a number of different angles. Some materials clearly take a particular tack, others use a more eclectic approach. Writing can be approached in a bottom-up way, sometimes known as process writing[39], where students start by formulating their ideas into sentences and gradually build them up into paragraphs and then complete texts (e.g. see Oshima and Hogue, 2006, Zemach and Rumisek, 2005).

Alternatively, it can be approached from the opposite direction, top-down, looking at examples of the text types that students are aiming for and analysing the features of

---

understood the underlying ideas and hasn't contributed much of their own in terms of analysis or evaluation. Their own voice and stance are often absent from such writing.

[39] **process writing**
Process writing is an approach to writing skills that involves starting off with a focus at sentence level and then gradually builds to paragraph level and then full texts. Compare **genre approach**.

those texts, sometimes called a genre approach[40]. Arguably, EAP students need a bit of both – to understand something about what they are aiming for and also the process of getting there. Below are some aspects of writing that activities might focus on:

Content
As I mentioned at the start of this chapter, unlike in a general EFL class where students are commonly asked to write about topics 'off the top of their head', academic writing is not about vague general ideas and personal opinion. It involves demonstrating real and often detailed subject knowledge, based on the students' understanding of their area and on information from academic sources. Replicating this in an EAP context, which might involve students from different disciplines or those just getting started in their chosen studies, can be challenging. In general, writing activities can either be based around students' own research into their individual subject or they can involve input on a topic provided in the materials, usually in the form of reading texts.

The former approach can work within the context of a particular course, for example, many pre-sessional[41] EAP courses at UK universities involve students completing a research project or an extended essay based on a topic of

---

[40] **genre approach**
A genre approach to writing skills involves looking at examples of texts in target genres (i.e. the type of texts students will need to write) and analysing typical features. Compare **process writing**.

[41] **pre-sessional**
Pre-sessional language courses take place before students undertake their main course of study, for example during the summer, to prepare them for their studies. Compare with **in-sessional** courses which take place during the academic year, usually at the same time as students' other studies.

their choice and written over a period of weeks. Materials can guide students through the steps required to choose and research a topic, and then to write it up (see e.g. McCormack and Slaght, 2005 and de Chazal and Moore, 2013).

Many writing skills materials though provide input for writing tasks in the form of authentic reading texts or sometimes lectures. Because of the difficulty of providing enough material on a topic which may be unfamiliar to students to form the basis of a whole essay, many writing activities instead use short extracts and focus on a specific sub-skill (as we saw above). Examples of this approach might include short reading texts as the basis for a summary or short extracts to be reported as part of work on citing from sources and using appropriate referencing conventions.

For students at higher levels, or later on in a course, a variety of short pieces of source material might feed into a writing task that involves synthesizing[42] the information. For example, in *Oxford EAP Advanced*, in a module about writing data commentary, we build up to a final writing task that involves both a pie chart and three short extracts (just 70–80 words each) from academic texts, two on exactly the same topic and one giving a slightly wider perspective. The task then asks students to not only describe the data, but to comment on and evaluate it, drawing on (and citing) the other sources.

---

[42] **synthesis / synthesizing** If you synthesise information from different sources, you combine that information (for example via citations) in a coherent way, making appropriate links to form a complete argument (written or spoken).

Alternatively, a writing activity can draw on input from previous materials (often in the same unit) including reading and listening texts already used for other tasks.

Style and structure
Once students have grasped *what* they need to write, the next challenge is *how* to write it. Here, two important elements are style and structure.

For students writing about potentially complex topics, organising their ideas in a logical, coherent way that guides their reader through their thinking is key. At a pre-EAP level, work on structure tends to revolve around the use of a few simple discourse markers; *firstly, in addition, moreover, in conclusion*, etc. Just by adding an appropriate discourse marker at the start of each paragraph though, doesn't mean that a piece of writing is well-structured or flows effectively. Els Van Geyte (in *Writing*, 2013, p23) provides an excellent example of typical overuse and inappropriate use of such linking words and advises that 'linking words can be helpful to guide the reader, but you should only use them if they are necessary; make sure you use an appropriate one, and vary their place in the sentence.'

Similarly, for students used to the fairly informal, conversational style of language learnt on most general English courses, getting to grips with an appropriately academic style can seem daunting.

A top-down approach to teaching these elements will look at how academic writers express their ideas and structure their texts. An extract from almost any academic text can be used to demonstrate basic principles at paragraph level such as topic sentence + explanation / expansion + supporting evidence or progression from general to specific ideas. As we saw in the reading chapter above, there are various techniques for highlighting these common patterns and helping raise students' awareness.

In the same vein, sample texts can be used to illustrate specific features of academic style that students aim to transfer to their own writing, such as the use of hedging language, more formal vocabulary choices or impersonal structures. This is often the point at which language work can be integrated into materials, which we'll explore in more detail in the next section.

Invariably, such activities start off by highlighting and analysing the features in the example text. They then move onto controlled practice exercises, before encouraging students to put the principles into practice in a freer writing task.

The choice of sample text for analysis though is an important one. As I mentioned earlier, authentic material from textbooks or academic journal articles doesn't represent a realistic model for most student writers (unless materials are aimed at the most advanced researchers or academic staff). Although some of the principles may be transferable, students can't be expected to replicate the style of an expert academic writer, and the structure and conventions of a published text will not necessarily be the same as those expected in a student assignment. In fact, the result of students attempting to mimic such highbrow academic texts can be muddle and confusion.

One alternative is to use sample student texts as a more authentic example of the target genre, to highlight and analyse relevant features of style or structure.

How To Write EAP Materials

Task 6

Consider the following questions:

1. What type of student texts could be used in writing activities? Who can / should they be written by?

2. How useful are either model texts (i.e. what tutors would be looking for) or flawed texts (i.e. those closer to what a typical EAP student might produce)?

3. What type of student texts have you used or seen used in EAP materials? How successful were they?

4. What are the potential benefits and risks of using sample / model student texts?

You can read a commentary on this task on page 117.

Stance, voice[43] and plagiarism
Academic writing in most English-speaking countries, especially at higher levels, is about more than simply repeating learnt 'facts'. Many EAP students, especially those from academic cultures where student voices are not expected to be heard, find it difficult to get used to the idea of taking a stance in their writing and take a while to find their own voice as an academic writer in English.

Many students initially perceive the concept of stance as taking a simple 'agree' or 'disagree' position on something. A better understanding of stance can be encouraged by including regular questions to identify the author's stance in reading texts. In this way, students build up an

---
[43] **voice**
A student writer's voice is what makes their writing hang together in a coherent, cohesive way expressing their ideas 'in their own words'; the style of writing that they develop.

understanding of the different types of stance that writers can adopt (which can often be quite subtle) and also of the language they use to express their position. In writing tasks, it can be helpful to explicitly discuss different possible stances on a topic as part of the preparation for writing, and to encourage students to note down their own stance (along with things such as perspective, purpose, thesis and audience) as part of an outline plan.

Voice is, in part, about getting to grips with academic style, as mentioned above, but it's also about how students manage to integrate ideas from sources into their writing and maintain a consistent voice. The difficulty that students have in synthesizing ideas from their reading with their own input – and indeed understanding where the line between these two lies – inevitably leads to issues of plagiarism.

Teachers frequently bemoan the problem of plagiarism and ask for ideas about how to tackle it. It is important that students understand what constitutes plagiarism and why it's so frowned on in academic circles. And a lot of writing materials do contain activities that explicitly address the issue, usually using examples of different types of plagiarism (some blatant, some subtler) for students to identify and discuss. However, perhaps more important in helping students to avoid plagiarism is showing them how they can combine ideas from sources appropriately, accurately and naturally into their writing. This isn't an easy skill and simply telling students to write something 'in their own words' isn't a terribly helpful instruction! Students commonly complain about how difficult it is to paraphrase or summarise a source because the original writer phrased the ideas so much better than they can.

Activities to help students incorporate sources more naturally include:

- Practice in taking notes on reading texts and using the notes to write summaries or citations without reference back to the original text, thus avoiding the influence of the original wording.

- Getting students to pick out and note down just a few key words and phrases from a text (you can set a limit if you want) and then use these to write a summary or paraphrase. This acknowledges the fact that, realistically, as proficient writers, we don't change all the words when we paraphrase, there are always some key terms that stay the same.

- Getting students to experiment with taking notes on both the content of a text and their response to it (e.g. using something like the Cornell note-taking technique. See *en.wikipedia.org/wiki/Cornell_Notes*) to encourage them to combine both reporting and comment / evaluation when they use their notes to write.

- Getting students to read a text and report on it orally to a partner, with or without notes, but without looking back at the text. This works particularly well where pairs have read different texts, so students are pushed to think about and communicate the ideas of the text 'in their own words'.

"Using sources is potentially one of the most challenging tasks for a student. Having various stages of note-taking and summarising can often be easier with lower levels than attempting paraphrasing."

Louis Rogers, University of Reading – co-author of *Oxford EAP B1+* and *Delta Academic Objectives*

Of course, any of these activities need to be accompanied by work on checking citations and references thoroughly, and keeping a note of reference information for bibliographies.

Feedback, drafting and learner autonomy
Whichever approach you take to writing activities, it's important to consider what students will do with their texts once they've written them. Different teachers and institutions will have their own approaches to giving feedback on writing, but follow-up activities in materials can be helpful in suggesting alternative approaches.

Editing is an important skill in its own right and one worth spending some time on teaching. Activities which focus on particular aspects of editing can help students understand how to go about revising and editing their own writing. Such activities might include presenting students with an unedited short text (a paragraph or two) that demonstrates a particular flaw to work on together in class. That might be:

- A text that is overlong, rather wordy and needs cutting down to stay within a word limit. This could be linked to language work on ways that academic writers make their writing more concise, for example, using long noun phrases or reduced relative clauses.

- A text that repeats one or two key words or phrases which could be replaced by synonyms (*plane > aircraft*), hypernyms (*plane > means of transport*) or pronouns (*plane > it*) or could be rephrased (e.g. using different parts of speech; *fly > flight*)

- A text which is too vague and lacks enough detail, explanation, examples or evidence to back up the points expressed.

- A text which is too bold in its claims and lacks hedging language.

Such editing activities can be created by 'reverse engineering' a section from a good model text to introduce a specific 'flaw'. Students then work to edit and improve the text and see how close they can get to the original.

In terms of students editing their own writing, short writing tasks are ideal for redrafting activities; it may not be practical or reasonable to ask students to redraft a 1,000-word essay, but a short paragraph or a single-sentence summary can easily go through one or more revisions in a single lesson. It will also cut down the volume of marking for the teacher – a practical aspect worth considering!

In an academic context, longer writing assignments will often be completed over a period of time and involve several drafts, on which students may receive interim feedback. Giving students ideas and techniques for evaluating and editing their own work and for responding to feedback helps them to establish routines that they can use beyond the EAP classroom to become autonomous writers. Such tasks can be as simple as creating guidelines, criteria[44] or checklists for students to evaluate a particular aspect of their writing:

Have you answered the question?
Does each paragraph have a clear topic sentence?
Is each sentence in the paragraph relevant and 'on topic'?
Did you move the reader from general to specific information?
Have you included comment and evaluation?

---

[44] **criteria**
A list of statements or questions used for assessing or evaluating something.

Is your evaluation appropriately hedged?
Is your stance clear to your reader?
Are all citations appropriately referenced?

Such activities can be aimed at self-reflection or set up as pair or group tasks. Either way, it's useful to present the checklists clearly either at the end of the section/chapter or perhaps at the back of the book, so that students can easily locate them and refer back to them for future writing tasks.

It's also worth thinking outside the box a bit and drawing on information and contacts within your institution to get an authentic perspective on what's expected of student writers. Many university websites include writing guidelines and assessment criteria and talking to subject lecturers can also be very useful. Bear in mind that different departments and even different subject tutors will have different expectations when it comes to student writing. In my own recent experience of going back to study at postgraduate level, I was surprised at the feedback I received on my written assignments from different tutors, some comments directly contradicting others! Giving students black-and-white guidelines about how to write can set them up for problems and disappointment ahead, so preparing them to read instructions and guidelines, to ask questions and to make use of tutorials or office hours is also really important.

> *"One tends to think in terms of authentic texts and tasks, but it is also really useful to collect a bank of comments from lecturers and supervisors on students' work. If you are writing materials, these comments can be used to frame tasks. For example, give a supervisor's comment on what constitutes a good or bad assignment or lit review in a particular discipline or context and ask students to relate some*

examples to these comments. It becomes much more authoritative and authentic than just vague advice about 'good writing'."

Jenifer Spencer – co-author of *EAP Essentials*

Writing Materials Checklist

Aims

- Does the writing activity have a clear aim and focus?
- Is the purpose and rationale for the tasks clear to students and teacher?
- Are you helping students work towards a particular student writing genre, if so, have you considered genres other than the traditional essay?
- Would a short writing task, or series of tasks, be more appropriate for teaching a sub-skill?

Input

- Have you provided enough input for students to have some real content to write about; reading extracts, input from previous reading / listening tasks or from students' own research? If you want students to research a topic, will this be feasible in all contexts?
- If you are working in-house, especially with ESAP groups, can you collect authentic writing tasks / assignments, examples of student writing, assessment criteria or examples of tutor feedback from subject tutors?
- Is analysis of a sample text helpful for highlighting features that students need to use in their own writing? If so, is an 'expert' text or a student text more appropriate?

Activities

- Have you considered activities to encompass a range of academic writing skills; incorporating sources, synthesizing, organisation, coherence, cohesion, style, stance, voice, etc.? (But not all in the same activity!)

- Do you have a progression of stages that build up to a writing task; planning, language work, note-taking, short writing tasks?

- Is the rubric / brief for any writing task clear; do students understand exactly what is expected of them? Would criteria or a checklist help students check their own work?

- Have you included work on editing, redrafting and acting on feedback?

- Is work on assessed writing tasks relevant to your target audience?

- Have you considered the practicalities of writing tasks for classroom management; silent writing time in class, group and pair work, facilities for research, homework, paper / electronic submission, marking load, feedback options?

CHAPTER REFERENCES

Argent and Alexander (2010) *Access EAP Foundations* Garnet Publishing: Reading

de Chazal and Moore (2013) *Oxford EAP Advanced/C1* OUP: Oxford

McBride (2012) *Patchwriting is more common than plagiarism, just as dishonest* accessed online: *www.poynter.org/2012/patchwriting-is-more-common-than-plagiarism-just-as-dishonest/188789/*

McCormack and Slaght (2005) *English for Academic Study: Extended writing and research skills* Garnet Publishing: Reading

Nesi and Gardner (2012) *Genres Across the Disciplines: Student writing in higher education* CUP: Cambridge

Oshima and Hogue (2006) *Writing Academic English* 4e Pearson Education: NY

Van Geyte (2013) *Writing: Learn to write better academic essays* HarperCollins: London

Zemach and Rumisek (2005) *Academic Writing: from paragraph to essay* Macmillan

4. Language Work

In what tends to be a largely skills-focused syllabus, explicit work on language can get squeezed out in EAP. Published EAP courses tend to either include language work integrated with skills activities, or sometimes in a short separate section, a page or two, perhaps at the end of each chapter.

Language work in EAP is typically around emergent language[45], that is the language that comes out of the texts and activities. So while a writer working on general EFL materials might start off with the aim of teaching, say, the past perfect tense or comparative adjectives, and design activities to fit around that aim, an EAP writer is more likely to start off with a more general rhetorical function, such as expressing cause and effect, or commenting on data, and then work on the language needed for this function, especially the language that emerges from the texts they use (written or spoken), expanding on and adding to it.

> *"Move from meaning (topic, writer's stance, main points, etc.) to language rather than the other way round."*
>
> Edward De Chazal – author of *Oxford EAP* and *English for Academic Purposes*

That is not to say that when writing EAP materials, you don't start off with an outline language syllabus. Language work shouldn't be just thrown in at random or 'bolted on'

---

[45] **emergent language**
Emergent language is the language (vocabulary and structures) that emerges from input materials (reading and listening texts), rather than a pre-planned set of vocabulary, etc.

as an afterthought. There are many important features of academic language that you would expect to fit into an EAP course and these would form part of the initial planning process for any syllabus. We saw in the chapters on reading and writing, many features of academic writing involve elements of content, structure and language choice. So, for example, work on critiques might look at how evaluation is expressed using hedging language (*tend to, largely, can*) and appropriate evaluative language (*significant, limited, effective*).

Many language areas involve elements of both grammar and vocabulary, so there's often less of a clear distinction between the two in EAP. For example, hedging can involve modal verbs (*can, might, may*) and impersonal *that* clauses (*it has been argued that ..., the evidence suggests that ...*), traditionally 'grammar' topics, but also adverbs and adverbial expressions (*arguably, not necessarily, to some extent*) which could be considered more as vocabulary. Looking at Ken Paterson's *Oxford Grammar for EAP* (2013), chapters include a mix of more traditional grammar topics (relative clauses, passives, conditionals) and many of these more functional, cross-over language areas (being emphatic, hedging, cohesion).

ACADEMIC VOCABULARY

For many students, finding an academic writing style is very much about shifting from a general, neutral range of vocabulary to the more formal, precise vocabulary typical of academic writing. Often this new lexis is not completely 'new' (although some of it will be), it's already part of their passive vocabulary, which they recognise and understand when reading, but not yet part of the active vocabulary they can use comfortably in their own writing. Thus, the role of vocabulary activities can be:

- to raise students' awareness of what vocabulary is (and is not) appropriate in academic writing.
- to encourage students to use more academic vocabulary, appropriately and naturally, e.g. through work on collocation, connotation, etc.
- to practise using vocabulary more flexibly – swapping between parts of speech is particularly important when trying to construct the more complex phrasing often needed in academic writing.
- to broaden students' range of vocabulary choices – especially in longer pieces of writing, having access to a range of synonyms can avoid frequent repetition of the same words and phrases.
- to teach the skills and techniques needed for students to continue to expand their range and to deal with new vocabulary they encounter in the future, e.g. through dictionary skills and knowledge of word formation.

What is academic vocabulary?

Academic vocabulary can be broadly divided into three levels:

- **general academic vocabulary**: vocabulary that's significantly more frequent in academic writing than in general English, and which is used across different academic disciplines (*significant, research, demonstrate, subsequently*)
- **semi-technical vocabulary**: vocabulary that's used in a specific discipline or group of disciplines, but which would still be familiar to (if not fully understood by) a general educated reader (*cardiac, gravity, macroeconomic, phonetic*)

- **technical vocabulary**: vocabulary that's very specific to a particular discipline or sub-discipline (*atherosclerosis, lepton, oligopolistic, schwa*)

General EAP (EGAP) materials largely focus on the first level of general academic vocabulary, with occasional instances of semi-technical vocabulary as it crops up in texts and/or is relevant to a topic of discussion. This helps students to develop a generally more academic style, especially in their writing. Some argue that with this base, students are more likely to pick up the semi-technical and technical vocabulary in their own subject area as they learn about the relevant concepts as part of their studies. Many technical terms are also more likely to have a one-to-one equivalent in other languages, so are more easily translated.

ESAP materials may include both general academic and semi-technical vocabulary, with only the most specialised materials specifically focusing on the most technical terminology.

The Academic Word List (AWL)[46]

One of the key tools which helps EAP teachers and writers decide which vocabulary to focus on is the Academic Word List (AWL). This list of words which occur frequently in academic writing across all disciplines was developed by Averil Coxhead using a corpus of academic texts (see the Victoria University website, *victoria.ac.nz/lals/resources/academicwordlist*, for the full wordlist and further information). The AWL consists of 570 word families, each 'family' includes words from the same basic root, e.g. *significant, significantly, significance, signify, insignificant, insignificantly.* The complete list is

---

[46] **Academic Word List (AWL)**
A list of core academic vocabulary used across disciplines, developed by Averil Coxhead and widely used in developing EAP materials.

broken down into 10 sub-lists, organised by frequency, so the most frequent words appear in sub-list 1 (e.g. *create, role, similar, structure*) and sub-list 10 includes the least frequent (e.g. *conceive, intrinsic, levy*).

Some EAP vocabulary materials have been entirely based around the AWL (see Schmitt and Schmitt, 2005) and many others use it as a basis, to a greater or lesser extent, for the principled teaching of EAP vocabulary.

Since it was developed in 2000, there've been a number of criticisms of the AWL:

- The inclusion of all possible derivatives in a word family means that some infrequent and rather obscure words appear on the list (e.g. *exclusionist, inconstancy, disestablishment*). Evidently, *exclude, constant* and *establish* might be useful to most students, but to spend time trying to learn the complete word families that go with these might not be the best use of their time. Note that the AWL website (link above) does show the most frequent words in each word family to help make more informed choices about which items to focus on.

- The AWL excludes the most frequent words in the language which could be considered part of a general English vocabulary (e.g. *the, person, go, take*). However, because these exclusions are based on a rather outdated list (West's General Service List from 1953), there are some anomalies, such as *computer* which appears as an AWL word despite its obvious frequency in a modern context.

- Because the AWL doesn't consider individual senses of words, words which have both an everyday and a more specialist academic sense don't appear on the list (e.g. *brief* and *party* have specialist senses in Law).

All that said, provided these weaknesses are borne in mind, the AWL can still be an incredibly useful tool and definitely a very good starting point for selecting academic vocabulary to focus on.

New vocabulary lists have been, and are being, developed that build on the AWL in different ways, although as yet, these have not become as established. They include:

- the Academic Vocabulary List (*academicvocabulary.info*) developed by Davies and Gardner based on the *Corpus of Contemporary American English*. Their website also includes links to some interesting tools, including WordAndPhrase (*wordandphrase.info*).
- the *Academic Keyword List* by Paquot (2010) takes a wider view of academic vocabulary and doesn't discount more frequent words that are also important in academic writing.
- the New Academic Word List (*newgeneralservicelist.org/nawl-new-academic-word-list*) is based on a wider (and arguably more representative) academic corpus than the original AWL and also uses an updated version of the General Service list (the New GSL).
- Work is also underway to look beyond lists of single words to multiword expressions used in academic writing, such as:
- the *Phrasal Expressions List* (Martinez and Schmitt, 2012).
- the Academic Collocation List developed by Pearson (*pearsonpte.com/organizations/researchers/academic-collocation-list/*) lists almost 2,500 collocations frequently used in academic writing

- the *Oxford Phrasal Academic Lexicon* (OPAL) (*oxfordlearnersdictionaries.com/about/wordlists/opal*) developed by OUP in collaboration with Professor Michael McCarthy is a collection of four academic vocabulary lists: written words, spoken words, written phrases and spoken phrases

A note on student vocabulary

Many EAP teachers latch onto the idea that students need to get to grips with the whole AWL (or other academic wordlist) to become effective student writers. This, in turn, leads to pressure on materials writers to 'cover' AWL vocabulary in their materials. Research by Phil Durrant (2016) though, suggests that even very proficient (native-speaker) student writers only use a small fraction of this vocabulary in their own writing. His research found that student writers only regularly used a small core of 427 items out of the roughly 3,000 words on the Academic Vocabulary List! This might suggest that while wordlists (based on expert academic writing) might provide a good general idea of the vocabulary students need for reading (receptive knowledge), they don't necessarily need to be taught in their entirety for writing (productive knowledge).

Tools for researching and planning vocabulary activities

Several AWL highlighter tools are available online for free, enabling you to input a text (cutting and pasting it from a document) to identify all the AWL words in the text. This is an incredibly useful way of selecting emergent vocabulary to focus on in activities that follow on from a reading or even a listening activity. In compiling the vocabulary pages for *Oxford EAP Advanced*, for example, I put together a mini-corpus of texts used throughout the book; simply all the texts pasted into a single Word document. I then identified all the AWL words in the texts, using an AWL highlighter, to provide the basis for many of the vocabulary activities. This mini-corpus approach also enabled me to check how words were used in context in the book, in terms of meaning, collocation, etc.

AWL highlighters

- The Compleat Lexical Tutor (*lextutor.ca/vp/eng*) – this site takes a while to navigate as it includes lots of different tools, but produces very useful results including colour-coding, a breakdown of all the words in the text (including the percentage of AWL words) and a breakdown of the AWL words by sublist.
- EAP Foundation (*eapfoundation.com/vocab/academic/highlighter/*) – this site includes a highlighter tool for both the original AWL and the New AWL (NAWL), as well as other specialist lists
- Text Inspector (*textinspector.com*) is a subscription site which provides a slightly more detailed analysis, showing AWL words by sublist and also identifying phrases from the Martinez and Schmitt Phrasal Expressions list

    "Use your intuitions but don't trust them: test them by researching the literature and relevant corpora."

    Sue Argent – co-author of *EAP Essentials* and *Access EAP*

However experienced you are in EAP, it's always worth checking your intuitions about how a particular word is typically used against actual data. The most obvious source of such information is an academic corpus. Unfortunately, while many of the major publishers have large corpora of academic texts, these are not generally available to outsiders. The BAWE corpus (*the.sketchengine.co.uk/open*) of student academic writing (already mentioned above) is available to search for free and probably more relevant to students in many ways than corpora of 'expert' published writing. Similarly, the Michigan Corpus of Upper-Level Student Papers (MICUSP) is a corpus of student writing at a US university. It's free to search and also provides interesting statistics about the distribution of words across disciplines and across paper types (or genres).

The British Academic Spoken English corpus (BASE, *www.coventry.ac.uk/research/research-directories/current-projects/2015/british-academic-spoken-english-corpus-base*) is the spoken equivalent of BAWE, made up of transcripts[47] from academic lectures and seminars, and allows you to investigate usage in spoken academic discourse, for example, for language work integrated with speaking and listening activities. As with BAWE, it's available to search for free via SketchEngine. Again, a similar corpus of US spoken academic English is the Michigan Corpus of Academic Spoken English (MICASE, *quod.lib.umich.edu/m/micase*) with a free online search facility.

The Corpus of Contemporary American English (COCA, *english-corpora.org/coca/*) has an academic section which you can search separately.

When looking at academic corpora, it's important to bear in mind possible skewing of results by specific terms or phrases that occur with a high frequency in a particular discipline. So for example, if you searched for collocates of the word *domestic*, you'd find *gross* and *product* coming up quite highly, as in *gross domestic product (GDP)*. While

---

[47] **transcript**
The written version of a video or audio recording.

some of these are easy to spot, others are less obvious, especially when they come from disciplines that you're less familiar with, so it's always worth 'clicking through' to investigate anything slightly unusual or surprising that comes up.

Several published resources based on corpus research already done by others can also be useful when researching vocabulary activities:

- *Oxford Learner's Dictionary of Academic English* (OUP, 2014): focuses on specifically academic uses of words, along with plenty of useful information about common academic collocations.

- *Academic Vocabulary in Use* (CUP, 2008): lots of useful semantic sets[48] together with plenty of collocations, and some really useful reference sections at the back on things such as informal and formal equivalents, common prefixes and suffixes.

- *Oxford Academic Vocabulary Practice* (lower-intermediate and upper-intermediate levels, OUP, 2017): focuses especially on productive vocabulary, including plenty of 'pre-AWL' vocabulary in the lower level title and reference sections on common collocations and dependent prepositions at the back of the upper level.

- *Oxford Learner's Thesaurus* (OUP, 2008): not specifically aimed at EAP, but lots of really helpful information when you're trying to tease out subtle differences of usage between synonyms, e.g. *important* vs. *significant*.

---

[48] **semantic set**
A semantic set is a list of vocabulary (words or phrases) around a particular topic (e.g. vocabulary for describing cause and effect).

Finally, any online search facility that allows you to search for particular words (or phrases) within sets of academic texts can be used as a rudimentary corpus. That might be a university library portal or an academic search engine like Google Scholar (*scholar.google.co.uk*). Simply search for your chosen key word and trawl through the examples that come up looking for usage, fixed phrases, collocations, grammar patterns, etc. Online academic journals are also great for exploring usage, especially if you're interested in more specific, technical terms or uses.

Task 7

impact   mental   observation   fore   behaviour

1. Use your intuition and experience to note down features of the vocabulary items above you might choose to highlight / practise in an EAP vocabulary activity. You could consider meaning, usage, whether they are in the AWL, collocation, typical structures, connotation, synonyms, parts of speech, word formation or anything else that springs to mind.

2. Use any of the resources suggested above to explore the words further and check your intuitions.

You can read a commentary on this task on page 119.

Effective EAP vocabulary activities

By its nature, a lot of academic vocabulary is abstract, and much general academic vocabulary has multiple senses and uses, dependent on context. So in vocabulary activities, context is key and it makes very little sense to teach it in decontextualized lists. Even presenting (or practising) academic vocabulary in the context of a single sentence can sometimes be challenging. Thus EAP vocabulary activities inevitably require longer sentences or even short extracts to establish meaning clearly and demonstrate authentic usage.

Authentic example sentences can however often be shortened to use as standalone examples in vocab activities by deleting extra information such as cutting dependent clauses. This maintains authenticity while saving valuable space on the page.

[original] *Proponents of the measure claimed that the increase would dramatically raise the living standards of the thousands of hotel cleaners and restaurant kitchen and wait staff – many recent immigrants from Mexico and many without health insurance who play a central role in the city's tourist industry.*

[adaptation 1] *Proponents of the measure claimed that the increase would dramatically raise the living standards of many migrant workers who play a central role in the tourist industry.*

[adaptation 2] *Proponents of the measure claimed that the increase would dramatically raise the living standards of many workers in the tourist industry.*

Another issue in writing EAP vocab activities is devising contexts in which the answers are unambiguous. Because the differences between synonyms or words with a similar function are often quite subtle, creating items which have clear right and wrong answers can be almost impossible. There are several ways of approaching this issue:

- Open gap-fill type activities have far more scope for different possible answers. Activities where possible answers are given, in the form of multiple choice or a choice of items from a word pool, can restrict those options. Although beware that in an attempt to create an item with a clear correct answer, the distractors don't become so unfeasible as to make the activity too easy.

Too open?
This article _____ the issue of the degree to which children benefit from smaller class sizes.

Distractors too unlikely?
This article tells / addresses / references *the issue of the degree to which ...*

Just right?
This article concerns / addresses / arises *the issue of the degree to which ...*

- Items where the choice of answer is dependent on the grammatical structure, a preposition or a collocation as well as meaning help to narrow down options. However, you have to bear in mind what it is you want to practise / check. If the structure, preposition, etc. are relevant and part of what is being practised, then such a technique is legitimate, but it should not be the determining factor where the aim of the activity is to distinguish between meaning or usage. In the first example below, the answer depends on grammatical fit (*permit sb to do*, NOT *accept / tolerate sb to do*). The second, however, depends on meaning only (as each of the verbs can take a direct object, but only the first fits with the non-human subject, *legislation*).

a. The current legislation permits / accepts / tolerates *shops to trade for limited hours only on a Sunday.*

b. The current legislation permits / accepts / tolerates *limited Sunday trading only.*

- Not all vocab practice activities need to focus on individual words. Activities can also practise collocation, dependent prepositions or other patterns which words typically occur in. That might involve matching sentence halves, where students have to consider both meaning and collocation to make the correct matches. It might also involve longer gaps which require more than one word, e.g. key word plus preposition.

- Alternatively, allowing for flexibility within the rubric can change a simple vocab activity into an opportunity for discussion. Students can be asked to choose the 'best' word (or phrase), rather than the 'correct' option to complete a sentence, and then explain and justify their answers. When opting for this approach, it's important to bear in mind the role of the teacher and the practicalities of classroom management. It's better to have a small number of items, so that discussions don't go on too long, and it's essential that there are clear accompanying teacher's notes so that the teacher can feel confident in giving feedback and settling any 'disputes'. This still may not involve a clear-cut 'right' answer, but commentary on how one choice over another might affect the message conveyed. Sowton (2012) suggests four main criteria for distinguishing between synonyms; context, formality, value judgement (connotation) and collocation. These could provide a framework for discussion about vocabulary choices.

Task 8

Evaluate each of the examples below as possible items in an EAP vocabulary activity.
- What possible pitfalls could each have?
- Would they be acceptable in some contexts but not others?
- Could any problems be mitigated by use of an appropriate rubric?
- How could they be improved?

1. The *economy / economic / financially* costs of invasive species total over one hundred billion dollars a year in the United States alone.

2. Although it is still not clear just how ENSO and other types of climatic phenomena influence the climate of the dry valleys, it is clear that even very small changes in climate can *assume / take / play* an important role in the ecosystem dynamics of the McMurdo Dry Valleys.

3. Family and caring responsibilities effectively *excluded / prevented / precluded* women from positions of political power.

4. Overuse of antibiotics can *cause / result / lead* in increased antibiotic resistance.

5. Nowadays, people in many countries ____ democracy.

6. In a similar ____ , Guest (2002) argued that a truly worker-centred approach will include family-friendly practices.

You can read a commentary on this task on page 120.

And of course, if your focus is on vocabulary for production, then you'll need to move away from simple gap-fills that just rely on students understanding which word fits best and create activities in which students have to actively use vocab for themselves. Receptive to productive vocab activities can be seen on a scale from simply choosing the best option (entirely receptive), to writing in words rather than just circling options (so that students have to at least think about form and spelling), to completing longer gaps, work on collocation, sentence completion and sentence transformations and longer 'free' writing tasks in which, for example, students have to write a short paragraph including a number of target items.

ACADEMIC GRAMMAR

Unlike in a general EFL grammar syllabus based largely around verb forms and tenses, as we have seen, EAP grammar tends to focus more on functions, and grammar and vocabulary often become blurred. That's not to say that EAP grammar is in any way vague or lightweight! In academic writing, language is used in very subtle and specific ways to accurately get across very carefully thought-out ideas which will be rigorously critiqued by readers, be they tutors or other academics. So understanding the effect of language choices, in terms of vocabulary or grammar, is very important for students.

Academic writing also tends to be denser and more complex grammatically than everyday English. Students need the tools to decode long, complex sentences and to build clear, but information-rich sentences of their own in an appropriate academic style. This inevitably involves some analysis and discussion of grammatical structures in EAP materials. As EAP professionals working in an academic context that values rigorous analysis and often errs towards rather impenetrable terminology, it's easy to get caught up in a level of grammatical analysis that is frankly baffling to the average learner. That's not to say that careful analysis isn't needed in order to write EAP grammar materials.

> *"Analyse the language you are presenting to a level deeper than you will need for the materials. This will strengthen your confidence and show you any complexities that might cause difficulties for the*

students in transferring learning beyond the immediate tasks."

Sue Argent – co-author of *EAP Essentials* and *Access EAP*

The challenge comes then in avoiding a superficial or oversimplified analysis, yet not going overboard with complex analysis and metalanguage[49] so as to confuse students.

Oversimplifications can mislead students and store up problems for later. For example, students often form the impression that in order to achieve an academic style of writing, they need to use lots of passive constructions. And while it's true that academic genres do generally contain more passive verbs than other forms of writing, passives still only make up around 25% of verb forms in an academic text (source Biber et al. 1999). Students can end up overusing passives in rather awkward and often confusing ways:

Two reasons for this trend will be discussed.
It is admitted that this phenomenon does exist.
For those students who talk to British people, their English will be improved.
[All examples from my own students.]

One way of avoiding this problem is to focus more on function than form. So, in this case, the real feature in question is the use of impersonal language in academic writing, which includes passives where appropriate, but also the use of non-human subjects; *the evidence shows, research has demonstrated, this approach results in*, etc.

---

[49] **metalanguage**
Metalanguage is the linguistic terminology used to describe and analyse language (*noun phrase, relative clause, adverbial*, etc.).

Note that the passive in the final student example above is unnecessary because the subject is already non-human – *their English will improve.*

And of course, a better understanding of why a particular feature is common will help students to better grasp when and how to use it – and when not to! So, impersonal language is common in academic writing in order to give an impression of objectivity and to focus more on concepts, trends, situations, etc. rather than individuals. Passive constructions are also used as a way of helping a text flow more naturally, for example, by putting known information at the start of a sentence – see what I did there? We'd already been talking about passives, so I made 'passive constructions' the subject of my next sentence, leading you from the already-established topic to the new point I wanted to make, about cohesion. To do that, I needed to use a passive, *are also used* – I made the grammatical choice for a specific reason, not just to sound fancy.

> *"It's important to remember that students are not applied linguists. Some materials spend too much time telling students about a feature of academic language without really showing its use, value or transferability."*
>
> Louis Rogers, University of Reading – co-author of *Oxford EAP B1+* and *Delta Academic Objectives*

However, presenting features of academic grammar in a way that's clear and gives students an accurate picture of how and why a particular feature is used is often easier said than done. Good examples, where possible in context, can go a long way towards illustrating a target feature. Parallel examples, that show the effect of changing a particular feature, can be useful in getting across subtler differences. Notice how the examples below and the accompanying commentary focus on meaning rather than form to demonstrate how the use of the target structure affects the emphasis of the message.

Active and passive verbs: changing focus
Compare the following sentences:

*King John **signed** the Magna Carta in 1215. It set out many rights which form the basis of modern British law.*

*The Magna Carta **was signed** in 1215, setting out many rights which form the basis of modern British law.*

The key focus of this text is the Magna Carta, so the second example makes this the focus of the sentence by using a passive verb form and leaving out the person or 'actor' (King John), who the writer decides is less important here.

However, there are contexts where the actor is the focus and so an active verb form is more appropriate. Thus in a text about King John, we might write:

King John signed the Magna Carta in 1215 after coming under pressure from a group of powerful barons.

~~The Magna Carta was signed by King John in 1215 after coming under pressure from a group of powerful barons.~~

Why doesn't the second sentence above work?

The use of metalanguage is a vexed question when it comes to discussing and presenting information about grammar. You clearly need some language to label particular grammatical features, but too much can just add to students' confusion rather than making a point clearer. The amount and choice of metalanguage you use will depend on a number of issues:

- The language level and academic level of the students.
- The target audience. In some education systems, language is routinely taught in schools using a lot of metalanguage, so students in these countries may be quite familiar and comfortable with a particular set of terminology. When writing for a potentially mixed audience (of students and teachers) though, familiarity with metalanguage can't be assumed.
- Usage varies (*present continuous* or *present progressive*?) and some terms can be contentious (what exactly is a *gerund*?)
- Teachers' knowledge of, and attitude towards, grammar and usage can be quite personal and can involve quite strongly-held views

There are a number of ways of getting round the problem of confusing metalanguage:

- Using 'skeleton' forms; *-ing* instead of *gerund*, *-ed* instead of *past participle*, *to do* instead of *infinitive*, etc.
- Using umbrella terms which cover several technical classes of words where the extra detail would be confusing (especially at lower levels), e.g. *linking words* to cover conjunctions, coordinators, subordinators, some prepositions, etc.
- Where a very specific language point refers to the use of a single word or phrase (e.g. *whom, of which*) or a small group of expressions, it may not be necessary to give it a further label at all.
- Glossaries to explain terminology – these can be either on the page (e.g. a small box in the margin) or at the back of the book for reference. More detailed glossaries can also be useful in teacher's notes, especially to establish the usage of particular terms.

Above all, it's vital to be consistent with terminology throughout a set of materials. Keeping a glossary-style list of terminology you use as you go along and reviewing it regularly can help to highlight any issues. Are you being consistent? Is the list getting too long? Have you used an umbrella term in one context then realised you have to split out more detail later? If you're co-authoring, are you singing from the same grammatical song-sheet?

Task 9

For each of the following terms:

1. Do you have a clear understanding of what the term means (be honest!)? Can you give a clear explanation and an example?

2. In what context would (and wouldn't) you use it in EAP materials? (e.g. language level)

3. What issues might there be with the term? (e.g. alternative forms)

4. Are there any ways it could be avoided or simplified without distorting meaning?

a. stative verb
b. modifier
c. non-finite relative clause
d. apposition
e. complex sentence

You can read a commentary on this task on page 122.

A final thought on grammar:

"Don't underestimate your students. If they are smart enough to be doing postgraduate degrees they are certainly smart enough to decode the grammatical complexity of academic texts."

Olwyn Alexander, Heriot-Watt University
co-author of *EAP Essentials* and *Access EAP*

Language Work Checklist

Language selection

- Is the vocabulary and grammar you are focusing on likely to be useful and relevant to your target students? Tools like the AWL can help you make more informed, principled choices, although remember they're only a starting point.

- Remember that intuition and received ideas about academic language can be misleading (e.g. overemphasis of unnatural discourse markers and passive forms). Can you use tools such as corpora or corpus-based reference sources to check your choices?

- Can you use emergent language from reading or listening texts as a starting point for language work? Remember though that the language of a published academic text might not always provide the best model for student writing.

- If you are writing for an ESAP context, how far do you want / need to go in dealing with technical vocabulary? Don't neglect general academic vocabulary and usage.

- Have you identified a clear language syllabus rather than just bolting on language activities ad hoc?

Language activities

- Can you integrate language work with other skills? If you choose to create separate language activities, do they link to other materials?

- Have you presented and practised language in an authentic academic context?

- Do activities explore more than just the surface meaning of vocabulary; collocation, usage, different forms, etc.? Just memorising lists of words will be of very little use if students can't use the language naturally and flexibly in context.

- Do activities really practise or test what you intend, e.g. can students work out the answer to a vocab question based on grammatical fit without understanding the meaning?

- Are the answers to activities unambiguous? If not, have you made it clear in the rubric and teacher's notes that there's room for discussion?

- Have you analysed language in sufficient depth to really understand what's going on? You may not include this detailed analysis in your material, but it can avoid possible problems later, e.g. as a result of oversimplifications.

- Have you made the function as well as the form of grammatical structures clear? Do students understand why this language is useful and when they can use it?

- What is the clearest way to present grammatical analysis to your target students? Can you avoid overloading students with metalanguage?

- Is your use of terminology consistent? Keep a list of terms you use as you go along and review it frequently. Defining how you are using terms (e.g. in a glossary) can be helpful for both students and teachers.

- If you are writing for mixed-discipline groups, have you provided opportunities for students to explore vocabulary and usage in their own discipline?

- Have you included activities to encourage learner autonomy, e.g. dictionary skills, language analysis and noticing techniques?

Chapter References

Oxford Learner's Dictionary of Academic English (2014) OUP: Oxford

Oxford Learner's Thesaurus (2008) OUP: Oxford

Biber, Johansson, Leech, Conrad and Finegan (1999) *Longman Grammar of Spoken and Written English* Pearson Education: Harlow

Coxhead (2000) 'A new academic word list' *TESOL Quarterly 34*

Durrant (2016) To what extent is the Academic Vocabulary List relevant to university student writing? *English for Specific Purposes 43*

Gardner and Davies (2013) 'A New Academic Vocabulary List' *Applied Linguistics*

Martinez and Schmitt (2012) 'A Phrasal Expressions List' *Applied Linguistics*

McCarthy and O'Dell (2008) *Academic Vocabulary in Use* CUP: Cambridge

Moore (2017) *Oxford Academic Vocabulary Practice*, upper-intermediate OUP: Oxford

Moore and Storton (2017) *Oxford Academic Vocabulary Practice*, lower-intermediate OUP: Oxford

Paquot (2010) *Academic Vocabulary in Learner Writing* Continuum: London

Paterson and Wedge (2013) *Oxford Grammar for EAP* OUP: Oxford

Schmitt and Schmitt (2005) *Focus on Vocabulary: Mastering the Academic Word List* Pearson Education: NY

Sowton (2012) *50 steps to improving your academic writing* Garnet Publishing: Reading

5. Listening and Speaking

In EAP, listening and speaking generally cover three main academic activities; lectures (listening), presentations (as listener and presenter) and seminar discussions (speaking).

SOURCING LISTENING TEXTS

Unlike reading, there isn't such an obvious body of input materials for listening activities available. If you're developing materials for use in-house and have a good relationship with other university departments, you may be able to make recordings of actual lectures that you can use for listening activities. Or you can at least sit in on some lectures to get a feel for the style and format of lecture that students can expect.

As with reading texts, you need to bear in mind the level and detail of content of a lecture when preparing materials for a mixed-discipline (EGAP) audience. Introductory lectures on relatively accessible topics will be easier to work with than very detailed, technical lectures halfway through a course. Also, lectures aimed at a wider student audience, such as on research skills, work well in an EGAP context.

There is, of course, a huge amount of video material available online, much of it relevant to an academic audience, from TED talks (*ted.com/talks*) to recordings of lectures from various universities, many of which have their own YouTube channels.

Issues to consider when choosing to use online listening material:

- Audio and video material are subject to the same copyright protections as written texts, so similar caution is required. You should check any conditions of use shown on the website and also the legal situation re. copyright in your own country or within your own institution before you use any material.
- Talks aimed at a general audience (such as TED talks) fall into a similar category as popular academic writing, in that they're intended to be entertaining as well as informative. Thus, while more accessible, they don't necessarily represent what students are going to encounter in their studies, so aren't always an ideal source to practise academic listening skills.
- That said, some public lectures, such as many of those available via university channels, do demonstrate many of the features of a typical academic lecture while being more accessible to a non-expert audience.

"To write effective listening materials, there can be no substitute for doing an analysis of the language the students will be listening to. For example, if you are writing materials for pre-sessional students who are going to embark on an Engineering course, analyse the language they will hear on that course, and structure your materials around building them up for that; in terms of techniques, study skills, accent and pronunciation, vocabulary and the grammar used on that course. To a greater or lesser extent, all materials can and should be driven from this authentic analysis."

Fiona Aish and Jo Tomlinson – authors of *Lectures* and numerous IELTS books

Academic presentations, which can be used directly for listening tasks or as a lead-in for presentation skills work, are more easily scripted and filmed using actors (or even colleagues).

When choosing extracts for listening activities in class, you need to bear in mind:

- the practicalities of timings during a lesson. A teacher (or students) won't want to spend a whole lesson sitting through a 60-minute recording of a complete lecture!
- activities that require students to focus on detail, either of language features or detailed content, are better with short extracts, just 1–2 minutes may be enough.
- activities that require students to focus on a wider topic may be longer, but are still unlikely to stretch beyond 10–12 minutes.
- complete lectures can be made available for self-study, for example via a website.
- if you choose to use just audio rather than video material, you may need to include any relevant visuals (such as slides) within your material.

LISTENING SKILLS AND ACTIVITIES

Listening activities can be broken down into two types; understanding lectures and processing lecture content. Students new to EAP may have little experience of listening to extended periods of formal monologue in English and can find following an academic lecture challenging.

Understanding lectures
There are several aspects of typical lectures that can be investigated in materials to help students get to grips with the new genre. In *Lectures* (Collins EAP, 2013), Fiona Aish and Jo Tomlinson start off with chapters on the purpose of

lectures, preparing for lectures, the structure of lectures, features of speech and understanding points.

Lectures vary depending on the discipline and level of study, and the approach and style of the lecturer. They typically follow a similar structure to other forms of academic explanation or argument though, with an introduction and a conclusion, a logical progression from general to specific (and often back to general), main point + supporting points and evidence, etc. They also tend to follow a limited number of general patterns. Aish and Tomlinson (2013) identify the following eight broad lecture types:

- cause and effect
- historical / developmental outline
- argument / modern thought
- process
- case study
- situation, problem, solution (evaluation)
- description
- applying theory to practice

Activities to raise awareness of these structures and the type of moves they involve can help students to follow the logical progression of ideas presented and to know what to expect next.

Similarly, recognising typical language features used in lectures, such as signposting expressions[50], can help

---

[50] **signposting expressions**
Academic speakers, in lectures or presentations, use signposting expressions to tell their audience what they're going to talk about next.

students break up that daunting stream of speech into more manageable chunks. When you sit down to listen to recordings of academic lectures or presentations, it's actually surprising how frequent and relatively predictable these signposting expressions are, so picking them out of your selected extract can be a fairly simple task. Some typical functions and exponents to look out for might include:

- Introducing a new point: *So let's start by ..., Now let's look at ...*
- Ordering: *So, Firstly, ...*
- Giving examples: *We can see this illustrated in ..., For instance ...*
- Referring to visuals: *In this table / diagram / chart, we can see ...*
- Focus / emphasis: *Today we're going to focus on ..., In particular, we'll see ...*
- Referring backwards and forwards: *So as I said ..., We'll come back to ...*
- Summarising / recapping: *So, we've seen that ...*

Activities to raise students' awareness of such expressions typically make use of transcripts (or partial transcripts), asking students to identify or classify the expressions used in an extract. Where there are few examples of a particular type in the extract you're using, you might use very short samples from elsewhere in the same lecture or go back to relevant examples from previous listening activities as a way of showing different variations while maintaining some context.

One potentially useful source for exemplifying particular expressions is the Talk Corpus (by Apps for EFL, *apps4efl.com/tools/talk_corpus*) which allows you to search for words or phrases used in TED talks. It brings up text examples from the talk transcripts, but also allows you to link directly to video of the talk, starting the video just before the phrase you searched for. For copyright reasons, it may be less useful for commercially published materials, but if you're preparing materials for use within your institution, it may be possible to embed live links or at least suggest searches within teacher's notes. And as always, corpus resources like this are a great place just to check your intuitions as you're writing.

Transcripts of listening texts can be useful for activities to highlight other common features of spoken academic language such as reformulations, clarification, vague language, humour and anecdote, etc. And of course, many of the signposting expressions that you highlight in listening activities can be revisited when teaching academic presentation skills. Remember that while there are many typical features of academic lectures that you can usefully work on, students also need to be prepared for the atypical; non-standard accents and alternative lecturing styles.

> *"Some of the most challenging spoken language encountered by students in higher education contexts is not 'academic'. For example, many of the most interesting and inspiring lecturers adopt a conversational style in their presentations. This often means using idioms, asides, anecdotes and metaphors that are not usually thought of as part of an academic style. Exposing students to this kind of language in teaching materials can be a valuable preparation."*
>
> Martin Hewings, University of Birmingham
> – author of *Cambridge Academic English B2* and *Advanced Grammar in Use*

Processing lecture content

The aim of academic lectures is primarily for students to access the content. Skills here involve pre-lecture tasks (preparing for lectures), during lecture tasks (note-taking) and post-lecture tasks (asking questions, using lecture slides or hand-outs, and processing notes).

> *"Remember that listening isn't just about listening. It encompasses note-taking, and non-verbal understanding, as well as critical thinking. Especially in terms of EAP, that means understanding, analysing and evaluating. Filtering information is equally as important as comprehending."*
>
> Fiona Aish and Jo Tomlinson – authors of *Lectures* and numerous IELTS books

Work around pre- and post-lecture tasks is often about raising awareness about expectations and techniques for getting the best from academic lectures. This may involve discussion or perhaps recordings of interviews with students and lecturers. EAP listening activities can also mimic the academic context, for example, by providing preparation tasks before listening, such as a reading text on the topic of the lecture, and post-listening tasks, such as follow-up reading, summaries or discussion tasks, especially those which encourage critical thinking and evaluation of lecture content rather than simple comprehension.

The main practical skill that can be practised in class is note-taking. Work on note-taking might include:

- discussion around the reasons for and benefits of note-taking.

- introducing and practising different note-taking techniques. No one technique will suit all students, so an EAP class is an ideal opportunity for students to try out and evaluate different techniques. Aish and Tomlinson (2013) put forward five main note-taking systems; simple lists, Cornell (notes on content plus response / questions), outline (with headings for main points and indented notes), mapping (grouping key ideas visually using arrows, mind maps, etc.) and charting (using columns with headings).
- work on common abbreviations, symbols, etc.
- annotating slides or hand-outs.

Perhaps most importantly, these activities shouldn't finish with just taking notes. In order to really evaluate the success of their note-taking or of a particular technique, students need to make use of the notes they've made. Such activities might include using notes to summarise the key points of a lecture extract, either orally or in writing, or using lecture notes as input for a discussion task.

SPEAKING: SEMINAR DISCUSSIONS

One of the most common complaints from subject lecturers is that international students don't participate enough in seminars. This can sometimes be partly down to cultural issues, for example when students come from academic cultures in which they aren't expected to speak unless asked a direct question. More universally though, it's down to confidence and the ability to formulate often complex ideas into language quickly enough to take part in a discussion. Students complain that by the time they've worked out how to say something, the discussion has moved on. Thus, materials aimed at developing discussion skills need to give students plenty of opportunities to practise and gain confidence in the relatively safe environment of the EAP classroom, but also to equip them with strategies to 'keep up' in academic discussions.

Perhaps more so than with the other skills, the direction and outcomes of a discussion skills lesson are very dependent on the teacher (especially their approach to classroom management) and the students (class size, background and attitude of the students, etc.). There's a temptation then for discussion skills materials to consist of little more than a question for discussion and a few useful phrases, leaving the rest up to the teacher.

Task 10

Evaluate the following materials for a discussion skills lesson. You could consider:

- possible classroom management issues.
- the relevance / authenticity of the task as preparation for academic seminar discussions.
- how appropriate the input vocabulary is for EAP students.
- the likely output from the students.
- the new skills that students will take away from the task.

Discussion task

Both boys and girls benefit from being educated in single-sex schools.

Work in groups of four. Discuss the extent to which you agree with this statement. Try to use some of the phrases below.

Expressing an opinion

In my opinion ...
In my view ...

I think / believe ...
I would have thought that ...
It strikes me that ...
It seems to me that ...
I feel sure that ...
As I see it ...
I'm quite certain that ...
My impression is that ...
I don't doubt that ...
The way I see it is that ....

Agreeing and disagreeing
I agree.
I (strongly) disagree.
I totally agree with you.
I agree up to a point, but ...
I couldn't agree more.
I wouldn't go along with that.
That's a good point.
I see what you mean, but maybe ...
That's right.
That may be the case, but ...

You can read a commentary on this task on page 124.

While much is down to the individual teacher and class in a discussion skills lesson, and a materials writer may need to build in a degree of flexibility to make activities adaptable to different contexts (e.g. large and small class sizes, lively or unresponsive students), there is still a lot that materials can do to facilitate a successful discussion activity.

Input

Input for any discussion task is vital to give students something appropriately academic to base their discussion on. General discussion topics, like the one above, where students are expected to give general personal opinions or base their points on anecdotal evidence may work as very early EAP tasks just to get students 'warmed up' and used to the basic discussion format, but they don't really prepare them for the context they'll encounter in their later studies where seminar discussions are likely to be based on prepared reading or previous lecture input. Students will be expected to draw on their reading and subject knowledge to connect and compare ideas, to comment on and evaluate sources in order to collaboratively build a deeper understanding of their subject. To mimic this, EAP materials should include some academic input for students to prepare before a discussion task. This can draw on previous reading or listening tasks, or it can be new input, such as a short reading text. Tasks early in an EAP course might just use a single source and gradually build up to using multiple sources to enable students to make comparisons, synthesise ideas, etc.

One interesting example of using a reading text to lead into a structured discussion can be seen in Tyson Seburn's *Academic Reading Circles* (2015). He proposes an approach in which a class is given a text to read in preparation for a discussion. The class is split into groups and each member of the group takes a different role, looking at and preparing notes on a different aspect of the text, which they then report back on to the group as part of a structured discussion. Aspects of this approach could be incorporated into various reading / listening-into-discussion tasks to provide structure and scaffolding.

Skills focus and pre-discussion tasks
As well as a topic and input for a discussion task, it should have a clear aim in terms of the specific skill or sub-skill that students are working on. Possible skills might include:

- turn-taking and participation
- asking for clarification
- discussion management (starting a discussion, including others, interrupting, etc.)
- introducing ideas from sources
- giving examples
- comment and evaluation
- recapping and summarising
- reaching agreement (e.g. in a problem-solving type activity)

Pre-discussion tasks can help to introduce these skills and to practise them in a more controlled way. Short recordings of student discussions (either authentic, scripted or partially scripted) can help to introduce useful vocabulary or expressions in a meaningful context. They can also be used to demonstrate typical features, such as the use of hedging language when disagreeing or being critical. If you're trying to script a sample discussion, it's worth either sitting in on some actual seminars if possible or looking at some spoken academic corpus data (such as BASE or MICASE) to get a feel for the tone and type of language that's typical. You may not want to replicate precisely all the false starts, repetitions and overlaps that occur in authentic spoken language, but neither do you want to present something too formal and 'perfect' as a model.

The Oxford Phrasal Academic Lexicon (OPAL) includes two lists of spoken academic vocabulary (one list of individual words and one of phrases) which provide a useful point of reference in terms of deciding which language to focus on in an EAP speaking context. The spoken phrase list is broken down by function, for example, phrases used for clarifying and restating (*as I said, in the same way, in other words*) or for marking a shift in or change of topic (*move on to, OK so, let me just*).

Picking out and learning to use fixed or semi-fixed expressions especially to start a turn can be invaluable in helping EAP students to participate in discussions. It gives them a 'way in', allowing them to take the floor and also giving them valuable thinking time to formulate what they want to say. However, as we saw above, it's important that these expressions feel natural and appropriate for the individual student. Otherwise, as with the overuse of discourse markers in writing, they can become rather awkward and far from fitting in with their native-speaker peers, they can make students stand out as overly formal, too direct or just 'odd'.

Observation, feedback and post-discussion tasks
It is, of course, difficult to predict what will happen during a discussion task: two groups of students with the same input material might react in quite different ways. For example, one group might get caught up in a lively and animated discussion, but one which slides mostly into personal opinion and loses its academic focus, while another might end up as a series of prepared monologues reporting on the input but with very little comment or linking. Thus, as a materials writer, suggestions for observation and feedback tasks often need to be flexible.

Having a final outcome as part of a discussion task can help to focus attention and produce a successful discussion. This might be a short oral or written summary of the points that arose, a written list of key points, factors, criteria, etc. or a final decision or consensus.

Observation tasks in which one student in each group is nominated as an observer can be helpful in raising awareness about performance. The observer should be given a specific task, related to the aims of the lesson, such as tracking participation (see below for an example of one technique I've used very successfully), noting how participants refer to sources or give evidence and examples. Such observer tasks could be included in the student materials or as suggestions in teachers' notes.

Observation task: One member of each group draws a diagram of the discussion group and marks each time a student contributes, showing who they aim their contribution towards. This builds up a pattern of both participation and interaction. From this example, we can see that Ben seemed to take the lead role in chairing the discussion. Most of the interaction was between Ben and Jason or Ben and Liz, with very little contribution from Phoebe. The observer shares the diagram with the group at the end of the discussion and gives feedback on what they noticed.

```
       BEN              PHOEBE
   ┌─────────────────────────┐
   │                         │
   │                         │
   │                         │
   └─────────────────────────┘
      JASON              LIZ
```

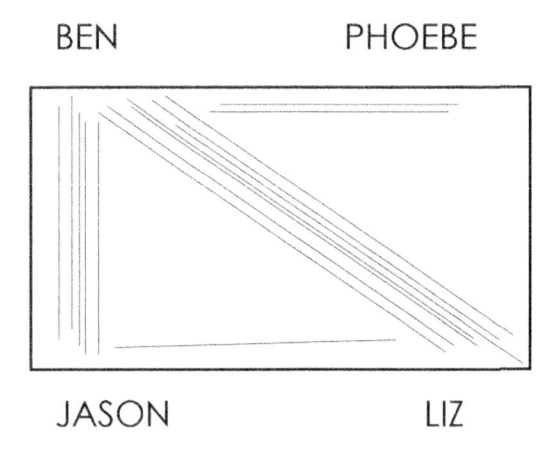

As well as feedback from observers and/or the teacher, students can be encouraged to evaluate their own performance using questions or criteria focused around the aim of the task.

SPEAKING: ACADEMIC PRESENTATIONS

Students will come across presentations during their studies both as part of the audience and as presenters themselves. Materials aimed at teaching academic presentation skills overlap with more general presentation skills materials you find commonly in Business English for example, but it's important to remember that academic presentations do differ in several respects.

Activities to practise presentation skills can be divided into two types; focus on delivery and focus on content. It's in this second area that academic presentations differ most from other contexts.

Focus on task and content
Unlike in other contexts, an academic presentation is generally less about communicating new information (except perhaps at the highest levels), but instead demonstrating your understanding of what you're studying (from your reading, lectures, etc.). Whereas in writing a weak student might get away with a clever piece of patch-writing – stitching together ideas from different sources in a way which seems superficially coherent – gaps in their understanding are more likely to become evident if they have to present their ideas orally, and most likely answer questions afterwards. This makes it important to establish this purpose clearly when practising presentation skills. Burton (in *Presenting*, 2013) stresses the importance of giving students a clear brief and narrowing the focus of the task. Are students simply expected to present 'facts' (description is likely to be largely an undergraduate task)? Do they need to add some level of analysis or interpretation (comparison, making links, applying theory to practical examples, etc.)? Or should they be including comment and evaluation, setting out a thesis and a clear stance (more likely at postgraduate level)?

Activities around planning the content of a presentation might include:

- understanding the task
- narrowing down a topic
- deciding on a clear message, thesis or stance
- organising ideas into a clear structure
- considering the audience and the level of detail / explanation needed

Such activities often involve analysing examples, either in the form of notes or outlines (e.g. evaluating several possible presentation topics to decide which are too broad or too narrow in scope) or as short video or audio extracts.

As we've seen in other areas, it's important for students to use some 'real' academic input for a presentation task, not just vague, 'off- the-top-of-their-head' ideas. They need to practise skills such as clearly explaining detailed, specialised or technical information, supporting points with evidence, introducing ideas from sources, developing ideas sufficiently, including comment, analysis, evaluation, etc. and this will only work with authentic academic content (at a relevant level). Again, this input can be researched by students and drawn from their own discipline (where this is feasible), based on writing tasks (presenting a 'paper' is an authentic academic task) or it might be provided in the materials in the form of reading texts, data, etc.

As with writing activities, presentation tasks can be quite short, especially in the early stages of a course, with students preparing and presenting just a single slide or one section of a presentation, maybe two or three minutes, before building up to a full-scale academic presentation of 10–15 minutes. Similarly, group presentations and poster presentations make good classroom tasks, involving plenty of communication and opportunities for students to learn from each other. They're less stressful for students than full-length, individual presentations in front of a large audience and often also more practical from a classroom management perspective. Poster presentations in which individuals or groups of students prepare posters which they present to small groups can work particularly well if the 'audience' then circulates allowing the presenters to repeat their presentation several times. Students often find that their first attempt is disastrous but by the third or fourth repeat, they've cracked it and learnt a lot along the way.

Focus on delivery
The other key aim of presentation skills activities is to help students to deliver the content of their presentation clearly, effectively and with confidence. Such activities will usually start with analysis and discussion of a sample (written, video or audio), followed by controlled practice and finally a practice presentation task. It can involve activities which practise the logistics of giving a presentation:

- timing
- producing and using visual aids
- making and using notes
- body language and eye contact
- engaging your audience (e.g. using rhetorical questions or familiar examples)
- handling questions
- dealing with nerves

They can also focus on the language skills required, such as:

- signposting expressions
- appropriate style and register
- pronunciation – an often-neglected area in EAP
- pausing, intonation and emphasis

As with discussion skills tasks, the final presentation is usually followed by a feedback and evaluation stage which could involve a combination of teacher feedback, peer feedback and self-evaluation, often guided by criteria or guidelines in the form of questions:

Were the visuals clear and uncluttered?
Did the presenter make the material engaging for the audience?
Did the presenter speak at a good pace and pause appropriately between points or to add emphasis?
Was the presenter's main message / stance clear?

Listening and Speaking Materials Checklist

Listening

- Can you source recordings of authentic academic lectures and presentations?
- If you are writing in-house materials, can you make your own recordings or at least sit in on some subject lectures to get a feel for the style, format and content?
- Do activities highlight the organisation and features of academic speech (such as signposting language) that can help students to follow a lecture? Transcripts are often useful for looking at specific language from lectures.
- Do activities demonstrate and practise a range of different note-taking techniques?
- Do activities require students to really engage with the content of a lecture and to ask critical questions, not just pick out surface details? Can you include activities that involve students using their notes after listening?

Discussion skills

- Have you provided enough input to prompt an appropriately academic discussion with some real content?
- Do activities encourage students to integrate ideas from source material as well as analysis, comment and their own evaluation? An academic discussion isn't just an informal chat about personal opinions and anecdotes.
- Can you provide a structure to discussions, especially in the early part of a course, such as allocating group members different roles in preparing for the discussion?

- Does your material highlight useful language and techniques to allow students to fully participate in an academic discussion; to start a turn and give themselves thinking time, to develop, challenge and defend arguments without coming across as too direct, aggressive or tentative? Be careful to avoid giving long lists of 'useful phrases' so that discussions just turn into 'discourse marker bingo'!

- Can you spend some time researching spoken academic language, by sitting in on real seminar discussions, browsing spoken corpora or making use of a spoken academic word list such as OPAL? Remember spoken academic language is a different genre in its own right, it's not informal conversation, but neither is it as formal and structured as academic writing.

- Do you provide opportunities for students to reflect on their performance in discussions, for example via teacher feedback, observation tasks or self-reflection?

Academic presentations

- Do students have a clear brief for their presentation task; in terms of content, length, structure, audience, etc.? Do they need to research content? How much detail and comment / evaluation do they need to include?

- Are presentation tasks appropriate for the students and stage in the course? Have you considered using mini-presentations, group presentations or poster presentations?

- Remember practicalities in terms of classroom management – there may not be time in large classes for students to give long individual presentations.

- Can you include sample presentations to highlight specific features of academic presentations?
- Do activities involve a mix of planning, developing presentation skills, rehearsing and giving presentations?
- Don't forget to include activities to practise asking and dealing with questions at the end of a presentation.

CHAPTER REFERENCES

Aish and Tomlinson (2013) *Lectures: Learn listening and note-taking skills* HarperCollins: London

Burton (2013) *Presenting: Deliver presentations with confidence* HarperCollins: London

Seburn (2015) *Academic Reading Circles* The Round (print and ebook)

6. Writing Better EAP Materials

Writing good teaching materials always requires skill and hard work. The complex nature of EAP materials, with lots of balls to juggle and perspectives to bear in mind, throws up its own particular challenges.

A key theme that came up time and again in comments from fellow EAP writers was the importance of evaluating and reviewing what you write at every stage.

Sam McCarter recommends keeping Bloom's Taxonomy[51] constantly in mind when developing materials. This helps you to try and build in activities that draw on thinking skills at all levels; remembering, understanding, applying, analysing, evaluating and creating. He also suggests that using a critical grid to evaluate materials from different perspectives both while writing and after writing is invaluable. Using this method you ask critical questions about the material – *Is the material authentic / relevant? What skills will students take away from the material? Does the material build on previous input?* – considering each one from different perspectives (e.g. materials / teacher input, student output, language load, content, etc.).

Of course, the questions you ask yourself will depend on the aim and the scope of the materials, but some of the perspectives or threads that you might consider when planning, writing and reviewing materials include:

---

[51] **Bloom's Taxonomy**
(first developed in 1956 and revised since) is a classification of thinking skills in the context of education. It goes from simpler to higher-order thinking skills – remembering, understanding, applying, analysing, evaluating and creating.

- language skills: range and accuracy of grammar and vocabulary
- academic / study skills: reading speed, selective reading[52], note-taking, etc.
- academic style: awareness and usage of appropriate register, hedging, etc.
- academic culture, norms and conventions
- critical thinking
- discipline specificity / opportunities for personalisation

What is the balance of these elements (in each lesson, unit, etc.)?

How well integrated are each of the threads?

How well does each thread develop throughout the materials?

How clear are the aims in each area, to students and teachers?

> *"When designing any activity for students, incorporate your rationale for it. In other words, build in the answer to the question, 'Why are we doing this?' so that it's obvious to participants. This is important for student engagement / motivation."*
>
> Sue Argent – co-author of *EAP Essentials* and *Access EAP*

---

[52] **selective reading**
With a large volume of reading to do, students need to learn to read selectively, choosing the texts or parts of texts which are most relevant or most useful for their studies.

It's common in EAP materials to include an explicit rationale or statement of aims at the start of a section or an activity, so that both students and teachers understand the direction and purpose of the tasks. This is also helpful for you as writer to keep clear in your own mind what you're trying to achieve and to look back on afterwards to check that the final materials match the rationale.

Getting outside help in reviewing and evaluating materials is also incredibly helpful in revealing what you might have missed.

> *"If at all possible, pilot your own materials (more than once) and encourage colleagues to pilot them as well. The more material is trialled the more likely it will work as you anticipate."*
>
> John Slaght, University of Reading – co-author of *EAS: Extended Writing* and *Research Skills and EAS: Reading*

> *"I think that EAP/ESP materials, especially if they are produced in-house, need to be peer-reviewed just like published materials."*
>
> Sam McCarter – author of numerous IELTS books and co-author of *Oxford EAP B2*

But you have to be prepared for negative as well as positive feedback. It's sometimes a good idea to give reviewers guidelines in the form of a set of specific questions or a feedback questionnaire to help them structure their comments and to help you collate and make use of the feedback. Bear in mind that there isn't always a 'right' way of doing something. Feedback will often be contradictory because all teachers have their own preferences, based on their specific context or experiences.

> *"Don't be put off by adverse criticism: unconfident teachers in defensive mode can be really negative. However, take it seriously: there is always a grain of truth in negative feedback. This can be like the grit in an oyster, forcing you to produce pearls!"*
>
> Sue Argent – co-author of *EAP Essentials* and *Access EAP*

Writing EAP materials can be very rewarding, with nice clear aims to work towards, often fascinating content to research and plenty of interesting language to really get your teeth into. It can also be challenging though, trying to get the right balance between authentic content and tasks, and scaffolded, well-paced activities which will be manageable and motivating for students. Especially when putting together materials for a whole course, it can be a difficult juggling act, taking into account lots of different threads while maintaining a clear and consistent direction and purpose. And a final thought …

> *"Don't underestimate the number of hours it takes to write materials for one hour of student effort. Some things come quickly but others take weeks of thought and revision. You should expect a ratio of at least 10:1 writing hours to student effort hours for materials to share with colleagues, and much, much more for publication."*
>
> Sue Argent – co-author of *EAP Essentials* and *Access EAP*

Commentaries On Tasks

Task 1

1. Differences between EAP contexts might include any of the following:

Place – university in an English-speaking country, university in a non-English-speaking country (English-medium or not), language school (in either context)

Students – mixed nationality or monolingual group, at 'home' or studying overseas, cultural differences, age

Language level – general language level on entry

Academic level – pre-university, undergraduate, postgraduate, researchers/lecturers or mixed

Disciplines – mixed-discipline group (general academic English), single-discipline group, e.g. all engineers (English for Specific Academic Purposes, ESAP)

Course format – full-time or part-time, pre-sessional (short course or foundation programme) or **in-sessional**

Assessed or non-assessed course – do students need to pass the EAP course for entry to their subject course or to earn credits towards their degree?

3. Which factors (language level, academic level, discipline, etc.) are most important will inevitably vary depending on the context and what students want / need to get out of the course.

4. One of the main restrictions on EAP writers is how much they know about the target audience / context. The narrower the audience, the more targeted the materials can be. Materials for commercial publication are inevitably aimed at the widest possible audience in order to make them commercially viable. There may also be practical constraints such as on the length of texts, the availability and cost of getting permission to use copyright materials, the availability of authentic audio / video materials, etc.

TASK 2

Just a few suggestions:

1. Teachers with a background in general EFL might come across a number of issues moving into EAP:

- Although they'll be familiar with a lot of the general language terminology (*present perfect, relative clause*, etc.) they may be less familiar with more specific academic terminology (*thesis statement, citation, stance*, etc.).

- While they will feel on more solid ground with the language-focused elements of an activity, they may be less used to teaching academic skills; identifying arguments and assumptions, asking detailed critical questions, understanding and using academic writing conventions, etc.

- In EFL the focus is much less on *what* you say, but *how* you say it. Teachers new to EAP often feel uncomfortable challenging the *content* of what a student says or writes, especially where they feel that they're not an expert on the subject themselves.

- In many EFL contexts there's an emphasis on fun and engaging activities, which are often short and snappy. EAP materials can seem long and dry in comparison and new EAP teachers often worry that their classes will be too boring.

2. Conversely, teachers coming into EAP from an academic background teaching other subjects face different challenges:

- While much of the academic terminology and conventions will be familiar, they may not be used to analysing and explaining the specific language used to express particular functions, and grammatical terminology may be unfamiliar.

- They may be used to a more lecturing, less interactive style of teaching and elements of classroom management, such as putting students into pairs and groups, may be new to them.

- As experts in their own subject area, they may also feel uncomfortable dealing with unfamiliar topics outside their own discipline.

Task 3

Of course, many of these features can be found right across academic texts. If you're looking for a good, reliable spread of examples, I'd suggest trying the following first:

- **abstracts** – for summarizing (especially the use of complex noun phrases to cram in lots of detail) and for thesis and purpose statements

- **introductions** – again for thesis and purpose statements, and for the author's own stance and perspective

- **literature review** – for examples of rephrasing and summarizing (of others' work and ideas), and referencing conventions, also showing different stances and perspectives on the topic

- **description of a process** – for examples of impersonal language (*the beaker is filled with ..., the liquid flows ...*) and expressing sequence and chronology
- **results** – for examples of data commentary and more impersonal language (*findings show ..., results indicate ...*)
- **discussion** – for examples of evaluation and hedging (*it seems significant that ...*)
- **conclusion** – for summarizing and, typically, good examples of hedging (especially to talk about implications, predictions, etc.)

TASK 4

Some pros and cons of reusing reading texts:

Advantages for teachers / students

- If students have invested a lot of time in getting to grips with a text, it makes sense to make use of it again, rather than throwing in a whole new text to read as input for a subsequent writing or speaking activity.
- Students can try to make use of the specific language and features they've analysed in the text in a productive task – good recycling and reinforcement.

Advantages for writers

- Most efficient use of time spent researching, adapting and analysing a text
- Most efficient use of time and money spent on getting permissions

- Efficient use of page space using a single text for more than one activity

Disadvantages

- The main disadvantage of reusing a text across several lessons is that students and teachers (and writers!) can get bored of doing the same material 'to death'.
- Especially in mixed-discipline groups, students will generally accept using input from a variety of subjects (if the relevance of academic features is explained to them), but if they find themselves stuck with a topic that they feel isn't relevant to their studies over a number of lessons, they can lose interest and start to question the usefulness of what they're doing.

TASK 5

2. Exactly what students are expected to write will vary between institutions and between countries (with emphasis on different forms in different academic cultures). According to the BAWE research, at UK universities, the following are some of the most common writing tasks in these disciplines:

Biology – methodology recounts, explanations (especially at lower levels), research reports, proposals

Engineering – methodology recounts, proposals, design specifications

Medicine – case studies, proposals, personal accounts of professional experience

Law – essays, critiques, case reports, problem–question (applying legal principles to a specific legal case)

3. Some issues around creating materials to teach specific genres:

- Lack of detailed subject knowledge by the materials writer.
- Not all of these genres are relevant to all students in a mixed-discipline group.
- Even in a single-discipline group subject knowledge among the students may be mixed, e.g. students taking different options within law or engineering.
- The nature of some of these genres make them difficult to 'dip into' for shorter tasks within the time restraints of an EAP class – you can't write just the results section of a research report, for example, without looking in detail at the context of the research.
- Practical issues around detailed input for tasks – it's possible to base an essay or critique task on some general discussion questions and one or two reading texts, but more difficult to ask students to produce a report on a scientific experiment, complete with detailed results unless they've completed the actual experiment.
- Variation in conventions, format, etc. between different departments / institutions – the more specific you try to be, the more difficult it becomes to generalise, especially when writing for wider publication.

Task 6

1. Sample 'student' writing texts can be written by a teacher / writer either using their experience to mimic typical student writing or to provide a 'model' answer. The advantage here being that the text can demonstrate features (either good or bad) as required for the accompanying activity. Alternatively, you may be able to collect actual examples of student writing, either by EAP students, or by their English L1 peers. However, if you want to use student texts in materials, you will need to gain permission from the student writer to use their text.

3. and 4.

Advantages

- Model student texts help students understand what is expected of them, both generally and in terms of specific features. They also allow teachers to demonstrate features they are looking for.

- Student texts, especially those by strong EAP students or English L1 peers, provide a more realistic model for students than 'expert' published texts.

- Flawed student texts allow teachers to highlight common problem areas and potential pitfalls. They can be less 'messy' than texts from their own students.

- Flawed texts provide an authentic context for students to practise the editing skills they'll need to edit their own writing.

Disadvantages

- Model texts can be seen by students as something to be copied in a rather slavish, formulaic way that stifles their own creativity and the development of their own 'voice'.

- Model texts, however well-researched, may not mimic the exact style and conventions required by academic departments (especially in different disciplines), so should not be relied on by students too heavily (as above).

- Flawed texts risk introducing errors that students may not have already been making and which may, accidentally, be perceived as 'correct' forms. This might occur, for example, if an activity is rushed and not all students are paying attention during feedback. Alternatively, students can easily forget which were the errors and which were features to be copied when looking back through materials.

TASK 7

Some suggestions:

impact – AWL, different senses (1. effect, 2. physical collision), parts of speech (most commonly a noun but also used as a verb), collocations ('effect' sense: *impact of sth on sth, great / significant / profound impact, have / make an impact, assess / measure the impact of sth* 'collision sense': *on impact, impact crater, energy, absorption,* etc.), synonyms (1. *effect, influence,* 2. *force, shock*)

mental – AWL, collocations (*mental illness, health, disorder, state, capacity,* etc. *mental and physical*), synonyms (*psychological, intellectual, cognitive*), connotations and usage (why '*a patient with mental health problems*' is now more acceptable than '*a mental patient*'), as part of a set of perspective adjectives (*from a mental / physical / social, etc. perspective*)

observation – not AWL, senses (1. watching, esp. as a research method, 2. a comment / remark), grammar (countable and uncountable uses), word formation (*-tion* as common noun ending for abstract nouns), parts of speech, register (*observe / observation* more academic than *watch, look at,* etc.)

fore – not AWL, almost always used as part of idioms *be / come / bring to the fore*, except in biology/zoology *fore and hind limbs*

behaviour – not AWL, US vs UK spelling, grammar (generally uncountable in everyday usage, but commonly countable in specific academic contexts), different usage between disciplines as shown by collocates (*disruptive / antisocial / violent behaviour, learned / adaptive behaviour, social / organisational / consumer behaviour, behaviour of a cell / material / electron*)

TASK 8

Any evaluation is obviously subjective and much will depend on context (language level, academic level, type of course, etc.), but below are some suggested issues and fixes:

1. The *economy / economic / financially* costs of invasive species total over one hundred billion dollars a year in the United States alone.

A good example sentence – not too long, but enough context to make sense in isolation. The clue *over one hundred billion dollars* helps to give context to the target vocab. The answer is completely dependent on grammar rather than meaning, which is fine if this follows on from work on parts of speech, but not if the aim is to check the (tricky) distinction between *financial* and *economic*. To check / practise this distinction, you would need to use the same parts of speech and choose an example and context where only one of the two clearly fits.

2. Although it is still not clear just how ENSO and other types of climatic phenomena influence the climate of the dry valleys, it is clear that even very small changes in climate can *assume / take / play* an important role in the ecosystem dynamics of the McMurdo Dry Valleys.

This example is clearly too long and complex to check what is a fairly simple collocation (*play a role*). It could be cut down considerably: *It is clear that even very small changes in climate can assume / take / play an important role in ecosystem dynamics.* Also, as each of the verb options are possible collocates of *role*, it might be a good case for including *give reasons* in the rubric, or at least as a suggestion in the teacher's notes. (*assume a role* and *take a role* are usually only used with human subjects).

3. Family and caring responsibilities effectively *excluded / prevented / precluded* women from positions of political power.

The differences here are subtle, making this difficult to answer. *Prevented* can be discounted on grammatical grounds, but both *excluded* and *precluded* are possible with subtly different emphasis. At a fairly advanced level, this might be a candidate for a discussion-type rubric – along with very clear teacher's notes as this is a tricky distinction even for a proficient speaker.

4. Overuse of antibiotics can *cause / result / lead* in increased antibiotic resistance.

The choice here is very clearly dependent on the preposition *in*. Again, this would be fine if the focus is on prepositions and usage rather than meaning, although it could become fairly mechanical if it followed directly on from a presentation on verb + preposition combinations used to describe cause and effect (*result in, lead to, contribute to, account for,* etc.).

5. Nowadays, people in many countries _____ democracy.

This is both very vague and far too open – a whole range of verbs could fit here (*seek, enjoy, promote, support, are fighting for, are denied*, etc.) In style, the sentence is also more typical of a high-school essay than good academic writing and not a good model.

6. In a similar _____ , Guest (2002) argued that a truly worker-centred approach will include family-friendly practices.

This item is clearly targeting the fixed expression *in a similar vein* (an example of an idiom common in academic writing). If the target expression is among a relatively small set of fixed expressions presented just before the activity, then this could be a valid item. Alternatively, it could be presented as part of a multiple choice including other similar fixed expressions, e.g. *in a similar manner / vein / way*, to prompt discussion about why the other two don't fit as well here (because they suggest similar actions rather than similar topics or lines of argument).

TASK 9

Up-front admission: I had to look these up to check a. that I'd understood them correctly and b. whether others understand them in the same way as me. Grammar knowledge tends to be personal so is always worth double-checking against other sources.

a. **stative verb**
Sometimes called a *state verb* (or in some contexts a *copula verb*).

This is a relatively restricted set of verbs, so it may be simpler to give a list, or to describe the type of verb rather than use terminology

b. modifier

The concept of *modification* is quite broad, so a *modifier* can be any word or phrase which *modifies*, or gives more information about, another. It could be an adjective (a *large* building), a prepositional phrase (a building *in the centre of town*) or another dependent structure (a building *full of people*, a building *used for meetings*, etc.). Its flexibility makes it quite a useful term, but also a potentially confusing one for students – they get the idea that a modifier is an adjective, then suddenly it's something else!

c. non-finite relative clause

With the complex sentences typical of academic English, it's often unavoidable to talk about *clauses*. How much detail you go into specifying exactly which type of clause is being used will depend on whether it's important or relevant to the context. In many contexts, just *clause* or *relative clause* will be sufficient.

d. apposition

This is a fancy name for a relatively simple feature (where two noun phrases that refer to the same thing appear together; *Canadian author, Alice Munro* or *desalination, the process by which salt is removed from seawater, is …*).

It may be a useful feature to highlight in EAP materials, as a simple way of adding extra information, but it probably doesn't merit overloading students with extra terminology.

e. complex sentence

The word *complex* is often used to describe academic language in its more general sense (i.e. made of many connected parts; difficult to understand), but its specific grammatical usage here refers to a sentence which contains dependent clauses.

I know that for some EAP teachers, explaining the difference between a *simple*, a *compound* and a *complex* sentence is one of their first grammar lessons. I have to admit that personally, I don't think I've ever explained it to a class or used in it materials.

TASK 10

Possible classroom management issues

- The size of discussion groups will vary depending on class size and teacher's preference. Stating an exact group size can cause problems, you could give a range (e.g. 4–6) or just say 'Work in groups' and leave it up to the teacher to decide.

- There are no instructions about the intended length of the discussion task (e.g. allow five minutes) or how it should be organised (e.g. should one student get things started and/or act as chair?); these can be useful in teacher's notes.

- There's no lead-in or instructions about whether/how the vocabulary should be introduced.

Relevance / authenticity of the task

- The discussion question here is very vague and not clearly academic in nature, is it intended to be from the perspective of Education, Psychology, Sociology?

- Academic seminar discussions are typically based on input (reading or lectures) which students can draw on in the discussion (see later section on 'input') – this type of vague question with no input or preparation is not very authentic and lends itself to only a rather informal discussion of personal opinions and experiences.

- That said, this type of simple discussion question on a familiar topic might be useful as an activity early on in an EAP course to help students 'warm up', to get used to speaking in front of their peers, to practise basic turn-taking, etc. There is sometimes a place for 'inauthentic' tasks when they have a clear pedagogic aim!

Input vocabulary

- My first reaction is that there's just too much here. If you give a student a page of 'useful expressions' to use, they're liable to spend the whole activity reading through the list and not really taking part in the discussion!

- The expressions are decontextualised and not differentiated in any way. How are students to know which expressions are appropriate in which contexts? What are the differences in meaning / usage / connotation between *I feel certain that* and *I don't doubt that*?

- Some of these expressions seem rather stilted and probably inappropriate in a student discussion. Remember that EAP students are likely to be in their late teens or early twenties and the vocabulary of their peers is more likely to be of the *Yeah, but, y'know ...* kind than the careful formulations of a middle-aged academic! A search of two corpora of spoken academic English (BASE and MICASE) came up with no examples at all of *I couldn't agree more*.

- Similarly, expressions that might appear too direct or abrupt need to be treated with care. *I strongly disagree* could be potentially quite offensive if delivered inappropriately. In fact, the only examples of *I* +

disagree on the BASE corpus are *I don't disagree with you* and *I wouldn't disagree with you* – which I think demonstrate some interesting features of hedging and politeness in academic discussion.

Student output

How students respond to this task could of course vary greatly and may depend very much on teacher input beyond the materials on the page.

- It could, however, quite easily develop into a rather informal chat about their own school experiences, perhaps punctuated, when they remember, by the expressions they've been given.
- The way the vocabulary is presented suggests that students should give their opinions and then agree or disagree with each other, which could become rather formulaic.
- Students in some cultures might be rather baffled by the topic, especially if their own country has either all mixed or all single-sex schools. This will give them very little to draw on to make a meaningful discussion. It's important to consider the possible social context when writing for an unknown audience.

Learning outcomes

- As mentioned above, simple tasks like this can be useful for just getting students talking and used to participating in discussions.
- This type of simple task could also be used by the teacher to encourage critical thinking, for example, a good teacher monitoring or giving feedback on this task might question some of the students' assumptions and beliefs, put forward alternative perspectives, play

devil's advocate or ask how they could find more evidence to support their arguments.

- However, repeated activities like this are unlikely to move students closer to being able to participate in real academic discussions.
- Students might remember some of the expressions presented here to reuse in future discussion tasks, although it might then be up to the teacher to give feedback on how appropriate their usage is.

Glossary

abstract
An abstract is a short summary of the contents of a text. Abstracts appear at the start of **academic journal** articles and some longer pieces of student writing to give the reader a quick overview and to help them decide whether to read the full text.

academic level
A student's academic level, is the stage they have reached in their academic studies, i.e. pre-university, undergraduate, or postgraduate.

Academic Word List (AWL)
A list of core academic vocabulary used across disciplines, developed by Averil Coxhead and widely used in developing EAP materials.

Bloom's Taxonomy
Bloom's Taxonomy (first developed in 1956 and revised since) is a classification of thinking skills in the context of education. It goes from simpler to higher-order thinking skills – remembering, understanding, applying, analysing, evaluating and creating.

copyright
The person or organization that owns the copyright of a text (or other published material) is the only person who has the legal right to publish it. If you want to reuse a published text, you must ask the copyright holder's **permission**.

corpus
A corpus is an electronic database of language which is used to research usage. A corpus can represent the language as a whole or a specific area of language such as Academic

English. Corpus research helps inform a lot of modern language teaching materials.

creative commons
If a text (or other published material) has a creative commons notice (indicated by the cc symbol), this means that the creators have specified particular rights of use, often making it freely available to be copied or adapted without the need to apply for **permission.**

criteria
A list of statements or questions used for assessing or evaluating something.

critical thinking
Critical thinking is the process of analysing, interpreting and evaluating information. It often involves asking critical questions about the accuracy, reliability or relevance of information in a written or spoken text and making links between different sources.

critique
A critique is a written or spoken evaluation of a text, a theory, method, case, etc. As a genre, critiques are a common form of student writing across disciplines, especially at higher levels. Also known as a critical response or review.

discourse
Discourse is a general term to refer to all the features of language that are used to communicate in a particular written or spoken context. That can include vocabulary, structure, norms and conventions.

EAP
English for Academic Purposes: for students using English as a medium of study at university level

EGAP
English for General Academic Purposes: aimed at students from any academic discipline

emergent language
Emergent language is the language (vocabulary and structures) that emerges from input materials (reading and listening texts), rather than a pre-planned set of vocabulary, etc.

ESAP
English for Specific Academic Purposes: aimed at students from a specific academic discipline, e.g. English for law students

genre
A genre is a particular form or style of written or spoken text with its own particular features; such as a student essay, an academic journal article, a textbook, a lab report, etc.

genre approach
A genre approach to writing skills involves looking at examples of texts in target genres (i.e. the type of texts students will need to write) and analysing typical features. Compare **process writing**.

glossary
A list of terms and definitions or explanations like this! Glossaries can be used with reading texts to help students with difficult terms, vocabulary or cultural references.

hedging language
Hedging or hedging language is used to soften the impact of a statement or claim, making is more cautious or measured. Modal verbs (*could, may, can*) and adverbs

(*approximately, typically, sometimes*) are typical examples of hedging language.

information literacy
Information literacy is the ability to find, evaluate and effectively use information relevant to a task. It is particularly relevant to EAP students searching for information either online or in a university library.

in-house
If you are writing materials for in-house use, they will be used within your own institution, not sold commercially. In terms of commercial publishing, in-house staff are those employed by the publisher, as compared with freelancers.

in-sessional
In-sessional language courses take place during the academic year, usually at the same time students' other studies. Compare with **pre-sessional**.

jagged profile
A student with a jagged profile has a high level of skill in some areas, but is much weaker in others, e.g. strong written English, but poor spoken skills, or good general English, but little academic experience.

journal article
An article published in an academic journal. These are often based on original research and are generally a more specialized, 'high-brow' **genre** than academic **textbooks**.

language level
A student's language level is their general level of language knowledge and ability, usually judged on a scale such as intermediate, Upper Intermediate, advanced, etc. or via a general language test (such as IELTS or TOEFL).

learner autonomy
Learner autonomy is the ability of learners to continue improving their own language skills independently, especially using skills and techniques learnt in class.

marked language
Marked language is vocabulary that represents an unusual or stand-out choice by the writer or speaker. For example, a journalist might use a colourful idiom or a literary adjective to make an impact on their reader – the same vocabulary used in a student essay would stand out to a native-speaker reader as odd or out of place.

metalanguage
Metalanguage is the linguistic **terminology** used to describe and analyse language (*noun phrase, relative clause, adverbial*, etc.).

navigate
When you navigate a text, you find your way around it efficiently to find the information you need, for example making use of abstracts, content pages, headings, etc.

patch-writing
Patch-writing is where a student writer puts together sections of a text based on ideas from different sources but without linking them together in a coherent way. It may not constitute **plagiarism** (if everything is correctly acknowledged), but often suggests the student has not really understood the underlying ideas and hasn't contributed much of their own in terms of analysis or evaluation. Their own **voice** and **stance** are often absent from such writing.

permission
If you want to reuse a published text (or other material) you must get permission from the **copyright** holder.

pre-sessional
Pre-sessional language courses take place before students undertake their main course of study, for example during the summer, to prepare them for their studies. Compare **in-sessional**.

process writing
Process writing is an approach to writing skills that involves starting off with a focus at sentence level and then gradually builds to paragraph level and then full texts. Compare **genre approach**.

plagiarism
Plagiarism is the use of someone else's work in your own writing without acknowledgement. It can involve using the exact words or ideas from another writer without a correct reference. Plagiarism is frowned on in academic contexts and may attract serious penalties (such as failing an assignment). See also **patch-writing**.

rationale
A rationale is a written statement of the reasons for doing a particular activity and the outcomes it hopes to achieve.

register
The context in which language (esp. vocabulary) is most typically used can be described as its register; the tone or style of the language, e.g. formal, informal, technical, literary, etc.

rubric
The rubric is the instructions that tell students what to do in a particular task or activity.

scaffolding
The support that you provide for students in completing a task, for example several stages or activities which lead

towards a final aim, is known as scaffolding. More difficult tasks, or tasks early in a course might need more scaffolding to guide students step by step.

scanning
Scanning is a reading technique in which you scan a text for specific information, for example searching for a particular key word or phrase.

selective reading
With a large volume of reading to do, students need to learn to read selectively, choosing the texts or parts of texts which are most relevant or most useful for their studies.

semantic set
A semantic set is a list of vocabulary (words or phrases) around a particular topic (e.g. vocabulary for describing cause and effect).

signposting expressions
Academic speakers, in lectures or presentations, use signposting expressions to tell their audience what they're going to talk about next.

skimming
Skimming is a reading technique in which you read a text quickly to pick out the main points, ignoring details.

stance
A writer's stance is the position they take on the topic they're writing about; an academic point of view.

study skills
Study skills are the techniques and abilities that students need to develop for effective academic study. They might include, for example, the skills to read academic texts quickly and efficiently.

synthesis / synthesizing
If you synthesize information from different sources, you combine that information (for example via citations) in a coherent way, making appropriate links to form a complete argument (written or spoken).

terminology
In this context, terminology refers to the terms (words and phrases) that are specific to the teaching and learning of academic English. These could be linguistics terms (*noun phrase, clause, relative pronoun*, etc.) or academic terms (*thesis statement, stance, abstract,* etc.). See also **metalanguage**.

textbook
A textbook is a book written specifically for students in a particular academic discipline to learn about their subject.

topic sentence
A topic sentence usually appears towards the start of a paragraph and expresses the main topic of the paragraph. Other sentences in the paragraph further explain or support this main idea. **Note**: while the idea of the topic sentence can be a convenient teaching tool, not all linguists about the concept.

transcript
The written version of a video or audio recording.

voice
A student writer's voice is what makes their writing hang together in a coherent, cohesive way expressing their ideas 'in their own words'; the style of writing that they develop.

Titles in this series are ...

A Lexicon For ELT Professionals
How ELT Publishing Works
How To Plan A Book
How To Write And Deliver Talks
How To Write Audio and Video Scripts ↗
How To Write Business English Materials †
How To Write CLIL Materials
How To Write Corporate Training Materials †
How To Write Critical Thinking Activities ↗
How To Write EAP Materials †
How To Write ESOL Materials †
How To Write ESP Materials †
How To Write Exam Preparation Materials
How To Write Film And Video Activities
How To Write For Digital Media
How To Write Graded Readers
How To Write Grammar Presentations And Practice
How To Write Inclusive Materials
How To Write Primary Materials
How To Write Pronunciation Activities
How To Write Reading And Listening Activities ↗
How To Write Secondary Materials
How To Write Speaking Activities ↗
How To Write Teacher's Books
How To Write Vocabulary Presentations And Practice ↗
How To Write Worksheets
How To Write Writing Activities ↗

Our paperback compendiums

↗ *How To Write Excellent ELT Materials: The Skills Series*
This book contains the six titles marked ↗ above.

† *How To Write Excellent ELT Materials: The ESP Series*
This book contains the five titles marked † above.

For further information, see **eltteacher2writer.co.uk**

Printed in Great Britain
by Amazon